GRANDPA HAD A LONG ONE:

Personal Notes on the Life,
Career & Legacy of Benny Bell

by Joel Samberg

In memory of my father, Jerry Samberg,
the Rich Maharajah of Magador

Published in the USA by:
BearManor Media
P O Box 71426
Albany, Georgia 31708
www.bearmanormedia.com

ISBN 978-1-59393-722-5

Printed in the United States of America.

Book and cover design by Darlene Swanson of Van-garde Imagery, Inc.

CONTENTS

A Bell Grows in Westbury

I was awakened by my parents only twice when I was a kid after already having gone to sleep.

Once it was when Neil Armstrong jumped off the ladder of the Lunar Module to become the first man on the moon. My mother and father knew that I loved everything about outer space and would never forgive them if I missed that historic broadcast from a quarter of a million miles away.

So they woke me.

The other time was when my grandfather appeared on "The Joe Franklin Show" on New York's WOR-TV to demonstrate his latest invention: a pair of hot pants that steamed up whenever a pretty girl passed by. Mom and dad knew how much I enjoyed Poppy Benny (as my sister and I always called him) and that I would never forgive them if I missed his live performance on Franklin's popular late-night program.

So they woke me.

Sure, I'd be tired in school the next day, but I didn't care. Come on—my grandfather was on television! Which of my friends could say the same of their own grandfathers? Theirs ran rigging companies or owned candy stores or sold suits. Mine wrote songs like "Everybody Wants My Fanny," "Home Again (Without Pants)," "A Goose for my Girl," "Go to Work, You Jerk," "Two Times Tonight" and "Shaving Cream," which twice in his lifetime and once in mine had been popular on the radio. Perhaps not everyone knew the name of the man who was responsible for the song, but a lot of people recognized his words:

Our baby fell out of the window
We figured her head would be split
But good luck was with her that morning
She fell in a bucket of...
Shaving cream
Be nice and clean
Shave every day and you'll always look keen...

This was no ordinary grandfather. Ordinary grandfathers sat around grumbling about Social Security. Mine wrote books like "What Men Know about Women," which was comprised entirely of blank pages. Ordinary grandfathers fixed loose doorknobs. Mine drew up plans for eyeglasses with windshield wipers and happy greeting cards to give to people whose bosses have died.

Other grandfathers, if they weren't already retired, worked for companies, toiled in shops or factories, or were partners with other men in one business or another. Mine was an entrepreneur who wrote, recorded, packaged, promoted and distributed his own records—at last count 114 of them—and sometimes even appeared on stage or on television to sing them. Mine was the only one of all my friends' grandfathers with a stage name—Benny Bell. Mine never retired. Instead, he worked incredibly hard for more than 70 years trying to entertain as many people as possible.

Mine was the only grandfather who routinely made silly wordplay out of the names of all the kids on the block—"Kevin, Kevin, walla walla wevin, walla walla dinkle dinkle devin"—and offered strange and funny bits of advice, like

"Be well, if you have the time," or "Don't work too hard, if you can afford it."

Mine was the only one whose job was to make people laugh, and when I was a kid I believed that Poppy Benny was doing his job flawlessly, note by note and joke by joke. How did I know? Because I laughed all the time when he was around, and so did my friends (like Kevin Kevin walla walla wevin). Poppy Benny made laughter happen, regardless of the Cold War and the energy crisis or Vietnam and Watergate.

All grandfathers started out as children, though some were forced into adulthood early in their lives. Mine was born a child and stayed that way for the rest of his life. Which to my way of thinking meant that Poppy Benny was what a grandfather is supposed to be: just another kid, although with a lifetime of interesting experiences to share.

At parties, my grandfather sang his silly songs into a big silver megaphone while strumming an old, beat-up ukulele to which the megaphone was attached (another one of his 'inventions'), and to me it was a far more natural thing for a grandfather to do than sitting in a chair reading the sports pages.

Mine taught me how to play that ukulele. I sang his songs whenever the situation presented itself and repeated Benny Bell-isms to my friends and classmates whenever I could find a good opening. I figured if I could stay a kid forever, like him, why shouldn't I? If I could find my own true path and travel upon it as fittingly as he did his, I'd be ahead of the game.

There were always a lot of pictures of me in my parents' house in Westbury, Long Island, and also in their photo albums, but the single shot that always meant the most to me is the one in which I'm strumming an old ukulele and singing into a big silver megaphone.

Which is why the message my parents drummed into my head throughout my entire childhood was very disturbing and confusing:

"Heaven help you if you ever turn out to be anything like your grandfather."

MET BIMMIE THE HOBO

To be a Benny Bell meant to be spirited, witty, funny and sometimes a little crazy. But to be a Benny Bell also meant to be obstinate, paranoid, suspicious and sometimes a little hasty.

Given all the facts about his traits and personality, it is no surprise that one of the great mysteries of Ben's life and career is whether or not he *ever* stood a chance of becoming the famous Tin Pan Alley tunesmith and vaudeville comic he set out to be. Could he have been one of the select few to schmooze with Sammy Cahn and trade shticks with George Burns? Could he have been a card-carrying Friars Club member who regularly headlined in Miami, Los Angeles, Lake Tahoe and Las Vegas?

Maybe he could have. But he wasn't.

Instead, he was almost always broke and lived through more professional frustrations and heartbreaks than most people would ever be able to endure. He came close, but for one reason or another always blew it.

Many people measure success only in terms of fame and fortune, and by those measurements Ben certainly didn't make the cut. But does that really matter? He was the captain of his own ship, and seemed to enjoy the voyage. That's not always an easy accomplishment.

What's most ironic is that in the 1990s, the last decade of his life, there were thousands of Benny Bell fans coast to coast, as well as in

England, Canada and Australia, seeking news about his albums and won-dering where his next concerts would be. But by then he was too old and frail to take any part in the action. The internet had already become a repository of records for sale by Benny Bell (including Benny Bell and the Agony Trio, Benny Bell and the Mad Sohnians, and Benny Bell and the Catskill Mountaineers). He was a hot item. In the next few years cyberspace would make him even hotter, with song lists, lyrics, sound clips, interviews and biographical information available on such sites as "The Collected Works of Benny Bell," "The Demented Music Data-base," Wikipedia and countless others (in addition to several YouTube adaptations or comic visualizations of "Shaving Cream"). By the time he reached the end of the 20th Century, he was unable to do anything about the burgeoning new online or video technologies. He died with-out truly appreciating the scope of his novelty song influence, and that's the saddest part of the Benny Bell story.

Like many sad stories, it didn't start out particularly sad, simply because he was a happy child in a close-knit and caring family.

His father, Gidalia, born in 1869, grew up in Janow, Poland, one of six children of Shalom-Bear and Sarah Sandburg. Shalom-Bear died in 1879, at the age of thirty-five, due to a serious back injury sustained a year earlier during a friendly wrestling match. In 1890, Gidalia married Leah Gutteiner. Leah gave birth to five daughters, though only two sur-vived, Annie and Fay. Gidalia spent much of his time as a young husband and father in the Russian army (Poland was a Russian possession).

In 1901, seeking better opportunities, he traveled alone to New York City, where an immigration officer transcribed his name as Zam-berg. Leah, Annie and Fay finally joined Gidalia in New York in 1903, where he was making his living as a tailor and part-time cantor. On March 21, 1906, Leah gave birth to Benjamin in the family's apartment at 37 Broome Street, in downtown Manhattan. The attending midwife who filled out the birth certificate further complicated the circumstances surrounding the family's surname when she wrote little Benjamin's last name as Zamberger instead of Zamberg. However, the family continued to use Zamberg throughout Ben's childhood. (Ben eventually had it legally changed to Samberg when he was an adult.)

Another son, Sidney, was born in 1909.

In 1912 Gidalia purchased a grocery store and kept the family reasonably warm and well fed for the next several years. Other than the boys' bouts with the measles, the Zambergs remained in fairly good health through those first few arduous years as new Americans in the rough tenements of the Lower East Side. Their ties to the Old World were kept through faith (Gidalia made sure that Ben and Sidney knew all the Jewish prayers and customs, and he had hoped that Ben would become a rabbi) as well as through language. Only Yiddish was spoken in the home. Ben didn't learn English until he started school.

Gidalia was a strict but loving patriarch. Ben and Sidney's childhood indiscretions were met with the sort of stern discipline that the boys remembered in raw detail well into their senior years.

Finances were always fragile. The family moved eight times in the first ten years of young Ben's life, although four of the moves were merely to different apartments on Goerick Street.

One move, however, was across the East River to Brooklyn, in 1916, where Gidalia and Leah purchased a new grocery store in the Williamsburg section. But they sold it six months later and moved back to Manhattan. It was there, at 123 Goerick Street, where Gidalia died from pneumonia in 1917. He was 48.

Ben was a *tummler*—a jester and practical joker. He played many pranks, one of which he named in a journal as the "phone errand joke," and another as the "busted screwdriver gag," though we'll never know exactly what they were. With neighborhood friends he formed clubs, most of which were designed more to entertain than to socialize. He was fascinated by many of the characters who populated the Lower East Side—the bums, the peddlers, the shady people, even the poor, tired, huddled few who, for one reason or another, attempted or successfully committed suicide. "Met Bimmie the hobo," he wrote enthusiastically in his journal, as if he had just dined with the President of the United States. He also wrote of seeing drug addicts at the Essex Street subway station. He observed these characters keenly and committed their personalities to memory for songs and skits of the future.

The family moved a half dozen more times after Gidalia died. But Ben didn't let poverty get in the way of his needs. He saved hungrily in order to buy a harmonica, a mandolin and a few other instruments, and he got his more musically accomplished friends to give him lessons. In October 1918, at the age of 12, he took a job at the Odeon Theatre selling candy. It didn't last long. In August 1920 he worked at Paragon Slippers. That didn't last long, either. In October 1922 he joined the staff of the Regina Jewelry Company for a short time. Jobs were merely necessary evils to scrounge up the smallest of dividends to get him from one project to another, and to add to the household coffer from time to time.

He loved and cared deeply for his family. But sometimes he was just far more interested in watching the bums on the sidewalks of New York.

HOMELESS EQUITY

A few years ago I began an attempt to ride a wave that had been gaining a little momentum in American theatre—the ten-minute play movement. Many amateur, semi-professional and professional theatre companies across the country were beginning to put on evenings of ten-minute pieces and, having already written four full-length plays, I was eager to try my hand at the shorter format.

I wrote eight ten-minute plays, one of which I titled "Homeless Equity." It was based on an idea that popped into my head years before when I was commuting to a public relations job in Manhattan. It had occurred to me that bums and transients have always given New York City some of its color and texture, and that perhaps there should be some sort of union to help these people reap the benefits that their incomparable presence brings to the city coffers in one way or another.

"Homeless Equity" is about two people—a homeless person and his businessman companion—who try to raise money to build an organization that would do for indigents what Actor's Equity does for stage performers. (It was eventually performed off-off-Broadway by the Brief Acts Theatre Company in Manhattan in February 2008.)

Shortly after I finished the play, I took a break from my writing projects and started to go through Poppy Benny's papers and notebooks, which I had been keeping in a file cabinet in my basement. One of the first things I came across was a small, thin, yellowed pamphlet written and copyrighted in 1925 by Benjamin Samberg, titled "Hobo's Union." It was a tongue-in-cheek, eight-page rule book for prospective members of an organization for bums that was almost identical to the one in "Homeless Equity." I had never seen that booklet before.

Makes you wonder just what can be inherited beyond physical appearance. A thick skin? Cockeyed optimism? Stubborn persistence? Screwball ideas? And if that's the case, what about stubbornness, paranoia and mistrust?

As a child Poppy Benny had red hair, as I've had all my life, and that seems like a perfectly natural genetic consequence. But the urge to write something funny about a group of bums hoping to improve their lot?

Maybe my parents weren't so crazy after all.

A Swell Love Affair

Despite the heartbreak, the harebrained schemes and the mistrust that stifled much of his career, Ben had one thing that was a beacon of success, something that rose a million miles above all traces of failure: a love affair that lasted 67 years.

Throughout the annals of show business—fringe or otherwise—one would be hard-pressed to find a deeper devotion, a stronger bond, than the one that existed between Benjamin and Molly Samberg. No one will ever be able to take that away, and no one may ever match it. Even the great love affair between George Burns and Gracie Allen was marred by a little-known infidelity. But Ben and Molly were inseparable. Entirely harmonious. And in a way, the family was as proud of that as they were.

Molly Ehrlich, born in Manhattan on August 7, 1909, grew to be a hearty young woman who enjoyed tripping the light fantastic on the sidewalks of New York during the Roaring '20s. She was a pretty, robust girl with an impish look in her eyes and a naughty grin. She met Ben in 1922 and was smitten. Something clicked between the nutty, rail-thin, red-headed tummler and his hearty, impish, blue-eyed gal. Ben wrote her love poems and letters, and together they took spontaneous hand-in-hand trips to other neighborhoods in Manhattan. They exchanged little, simple gifts. He wrote a song called "Molly Dear" in March 1925 and another one called "Beautiful Molly" exactly a year later. When he proposed to her he was 17 and she was 14.

As Ben once wrote, "We were married in a civil ceremony on August 9, 1927 (marriage certificate #147664), followed by a Jewish ceremony on February 3, 1928 at the Rutger's Mansion, #9 Rutgers Street, Manhattan, now demolished—the mansion, not the marriage."

Actually, they would have had the civil ceremony a day earlier, but the application was rejected by the county clerk because Molly was one day too young to be legally married.

She never complained about her lot in life—the lot of being married to an eccentric, impulsive, comic singer-songwriter who only sporadically had enough money to support his family. Quite the contrary, she always seemed to enjoy his antics, from the songs to the skits to the marketing gimmicks and everything in between. She accepted him for what he was, and maybe he knew that he had the only women in the known universe who would. They had a love of family, a love of faith, a love of laughter, and a seemingly philosophical way of finding optimism and hope in the most pessimistic and hopeless situations.

Maybe that's what success really is. Maybe that's what success *should* be.

Nearly every time Ben was interviewed he made a point of mentioning the love of his life, even into his eighties. In June 1987, reporter Connie Collins from News 4 New York, the evening broadcast on the local NBC television station, did a story on Ben, and Molly was right there beside him. Their marriage had nothing to do with the story—Collins was reporting on a music video he had just produced—but Ben took precious air time to say how long he and Molly had been married.

Collins asked Molly what she thought about the music video and, with an impish grin, she told Collins that she thought the song was "swell."

Molly was a very bright woman who, like her husband, wanted to enjoy life. She had a lot of common sense. She had a good sense of humor. But if you knew anything about the life and career of her husband, you'd know that Molly had something else in abundance: the patience of Job.

THE CORNER OF DELANCEY AND FIRST

When he was eighty-three years old, Poppy Benny tried to pick a little fight with Jackie Mason.

In 1989 he wrote and copyrighted an article called "Jackie Mason According to Me" which gently chastised the famous comedian for making an error while discussing certain streets on the Lower East Side of Manhattan. The title of the article was based on Mason's then-current one-man show on Broadway, "The World According to Me." Mason had written in an article of his own that the best egg cream in New York while he was growing up was made somewhere near the corner of Delancey Street and First Avenue. My grandfather's response was that Mason "probably meant Delancey and Allen Street, which becomes First Avenue three blocks north on East Houston Street."

Jackie Mason may have known how to fill a Broadway theatre, but Benny Bell knew the Lower East Side.

He tried to sell the article to all the New York City daily newspapers, but it was a bit too muddled and self-serving (the entire second half was a recap of how one of his most famous songs came to be written), and it was never published.

The following year, when he was eighty-four, he composed what he called "Witty Ditties and a Vaudeville Act" which, as its title implies, was an attempt to bring back an all-but-obsolete form of entertainment. There may even have been some merit there, since nostalgia goes through phases with varying degrees of success. But it would have needed a massive campaign to pique the public's interest. There is no indication, however, that other than writing it, publishing it and having it copyrighted, he did anything at all with "Witty Ditties." A year or two earlier he might have made a demonstration video of the songs and skits and peddled it to all the cable networks and television variety shows, ushering himself from office to office by foot, or maybe by subway, across his beloved New York City. But he was running out of steam.

Poppy Benny may have been silly, stubborn and self-absorbed, but he was wise enough to acknowledge that he wouldn't last forever, and wanted to make sure that his legacy was in safe hands. So shortly after he wrote "Jackie Mason According to Me," he started to give me stacks of old copyright papers, along with ledgers in which he had catalogued all the songs he had written, folders full of sheet music, boxes packed with comedy skits, clippings of reviews of some of his shows, ads from some of his albums, genealogy charts dating back to the late 1800s, and books of old family photographs.

And, of course, records.

"This is very important stuff," he said to me the last few times I had visited him in his Brooklyn apartment. "Don't lose it. It's priceless. I want to give it to you now, while I still remember. Because I have a memory like a fish."

"You told me you have a memory like a fish last time I was here," I responded. "Don't you remember?"

"How can I remember? I have a memory like a fish."

And then he'd chuckle, showing the same wry sparkle in his eye that I had been seeing for the last 30 years, ever since I was old enough to notice such things. But that was really one of the only things that was the same. He had indeed changed. He still hummed, but the melodies ceased being instantly recognizable. He still told stories, but they were no longer entirely coherent. He had the memory of a fish. And he was taking more time than ever before preparing to "kick the bucket" by giving me his papers and records.

I admired that he could do that with such candor and good humor—yet at the same time it bothered me, because I didn't want to believe that he was going anywhere. We all know we're going to die, and that's never an easy lesson—but comedians have a knack for making it part of their act. George Burns always joked about being booked for years to come, making death a virtual impossibility. Buddy Hackett placed a sign at his gravesite that said, "Coming Soon."

Poppy Benny always talked about going to the big jukebox in the sky, where he'd finally get to play all his own records.

And shortly thereafter he did go to the big jukebox in the sky, where I'm positive he's arguing right now with someone who thinks that First Avenue crosses Delancey Street.

Oo-la-la, Oui Oui

When you have a grandfather who is always singing, humming, cracking jokes and making wry observations, it's hard to believe that he could have once been despondent, shattered by defeat and racked by grief.

Mine was.

Maybe all grandsons should find a way to visit their grandfathers when they were young. I imagine it could help put some things into perspective, particularly if the grandson has some interest in what was or what could have been. Then again, perhaps not many grandsons have that desire.

Why did he become a songwriter? With his love of Judaism and a singing voice that was most emotive when chanting in Hebrew, he could have been a cantor or a rabbi (as his father had hoped). Or he could have owned a grocery store, which had been a family vocation, and which quite possibly could have been a good way to guarantee a paying daily audience of adoring fans who would come into the store for eggs, milk and a silly song.

It was Irving Berlin, whom Ben had met just once in passing, who was responsible for the professional direction he eventually chose. In 1912 Berlin wrote a song called "When I Lost You" in memory of his

first wife, Dorothy, who died of pneumonia just months after the two
had married, and it was that song that made my grandfather fall in love
with music. Berlin, at 24, was already a legend in the business, having written the phenomenally successful "Alexander's Ragtime Band"
in 1910 and several songs for Florenz Ziegfeld's triumphant "Follies of
1911" on Broadway. "When I Lost You," which was Berlin's simplest
and most tender composition to date, was also a hit, and Ben remem-
bers it as the first English song he memorized in full. He was only six
years old at the time.

I must have heard him sing "When I Lost You" at least 200 times as
I was growing up—sometimes with ukulele accompaniment, sometimes
a cappella. He taught me how to play the ukulele with that song. He
sang it as if it were his own, and when I was little I thought it was. I was
a teenager by the time I found out that someone else had written it. He
never fooled around with the music or lyrics, as he might with other
songs. That song was sacred.

Perhaps it was also the fortunes of its creator, Mr. Berlin, that had
something to do with Ben's career choice. In 1921, when he was 15,
Ben read an article in a magazine about the incredible prosperity of
some of the nation's top songwriters at the time. Berlin was bigger than
ever, with current hits like "A Pretty Girl is Like a Melody" and "Say
It With Music." Other songwriters were equally successful. "Swanee,"
by Irving Caesar and George Gershwin, "April Showers," by Buddy
DeSylva and Louis Silvers, and "Ain't We Got Fun?" by Richard Whiting, Raymond Egan and Gus Kahn were sensationally popular songs that
came out shortly before the article was published.

Ben had already been trying his hand on creative projects by then, although on a somewhat casual basis. He wrote his first song, "A Toast to God," in November 1919, followed by more than a dozen others in the next two years.

The article sealed it for him. Why not make a living doing what he already seemed to enjoy—and what the wealthy Irving Berlin did with such apparent ease? So, at 15 years of age, Benjamin Zamberg decided he would become a professional songwriter.

In 1923, at the age of 17, he attempted to take his first real commercial steps by submitting one of his songs to Harry Von Tilzer, a noted songwriter who had become an influential music publisher and promoter. But Von Tilzer rejected the song.

Von Tilzer, born Harold Gumm (his niece, Frances Gumm, would later change her name to Judy Garland), had a song called "My Old New Hampshire Home" accepted by a publisher in 1898, which ended up selling more than two million copies in sheet music, prompting him to go into songwriting full time. He collaborated on many hit songs in the 1890s and early 1900s, including "A Girl in a Gilded Cage" and "I Want a Girl Just Like a Girl Who Married Dear Old Dad." He was also one of the first tunesmiths to found his own music publishing firm as a way of retaining more of the royalties to which he felt he was entitled. And he was instrumental in helping both Irving Berlin and George Gershwin get started on their own roads to success.

By the time the 1920s rolled around Von Tilzer had determined that the musical styles of the day weren't to his particular liking as a songwriter, and so he concentrated a little more on producing and promoting others, and that's when Ben approached him. It isn't known which of Ben's songs Von Tilzer rejected, but by that time there were at least 20 to choose from, with titles such as "Oo-la-la, Oui Oui," "Dixie in the Summertime," "When I Was a Kid" and "When He Took You Away From Me."

Five months after the Von Tilzer rejection, in October 1923, Ben received a positive response on some of his songs from a firm called the New York Melody Company. For just $45 and a signed contract, the company promised to produce and distribute his latest composition, "Till the Sun Will Fall Down From the Sky," along with a few of his other songs. But the New York Melody Company proved to be a less-than-legitimate firm, and the contract Ben signed was a fake. The money he gave them, a significant sum at the time, was gone, and his songs were all but discarded. It had taken him many months to save up that much money; the family had little income and meager savings, and as the oldest son in a household without a father, Ben had to contribute as much as he could, even though he was still in school.

There was nothing that could be done about the phony contract. No one in the family had ties to music industry professionals or attorneys who might offer help and advice on how to fight it, and certainly no one knew how to fight it on their own.

Then, following several more song rejections (including a rejection by Eddie Cantor), Ben approached another publishing company that seemed interested in his work, and while it wasn't one of the giant firms, it at least had a solid history. In fact, Bibo, Bloedon & Lang, Inc. (typically referred to as Bibo-Lang) would go on in the next few years to become the first company to publish a book based on a Disney character, "The Mickey Mouse Book," as well as the songs used in the 1930 motion pictures "The Jazz Cinderella" and "Ladies in Love." Bibo-Lang's cofounder, Irving Bibo, composed "Huggable Kissable You," which Rudy Vallee recorded in 1929, and the company published "Aloha Beloved," recorded in 1932 by Kate Smith.

Ben actually came to Bibo-Lang by way of the Velvet-Tone Record Company, which was a subsidiary of Columbia Records. He managed to get a meeting with Velvet-Tone executives Herman Rose and Ted Collins in September 1928. Velvet-Tone was interested in three of Ben's songs, "The Bowery Bums," "The Bum's Rush" and "Once a Bum, Always a Bum," each of which painted a colorful musical picture based on the kind of Lower East Side characters that had long fascinated him. He and Molly had gotten married only a few months before, and the meeting with Rose and Collins at Velvet-Tone was a cause for celebration. For him it was, potentially, the biggest step taken to date as a young songwriter.

But Velvet-Tone produced records, they didn't publish songs, and Rose and Collins stipulated to Ben that before the label could turn the three 'bum' tunes into records, the songs would have to be published. It is likely that Collins suggested Bibo-Lang as the publisher because he already had a relationship with that firm.

Bibo-Lang did indeed publish Ben's three songs, and the following year, while Molly was pregnant with her first child, Velvet-Tone recorded them with Hobo Jack Turner as the vocalist. Hobo Jack Turner was the pseudonym of a popular tenor by the name of Thomas Ernest Hare, who had once been Al Jolson's understudy on Broadway. Turner had had several hits—many of them labeled as hillbilly songs—on the Velvet-Tone label. Things were certainly looking up for Ben and Molly, and there must have been quite a bit of oo-la-la oui oui in their Brooklyn apartment when they heard Hobo Jack Turner singing Ben's songs on the radio:

I've slept on the stations
I've slept on the rails
On tables, in stables and forty odd jails
I've slept on a mountain
I've slept in a trench
But the place I love the best is the park on a bench

Chir-i-bim-bim-bum bam
What a big bum I am
I want you to know
I'm the best Hobo man

In addition to the Hobo Jack Turner recording, another of Ben's character songs, "Oh, That Dumb Bell," was recorded that year by Frank Luther, a popular country singer of the day. A songwriter himself, Luther partnered for a time with country star Carson Robison, whose band backed him up on the recording:

I never worshipped heroes
Whoever they may be
A royal king or hobo were all the same to me
Until I met a fellow, and to him I drink a toast
For he is no doubt the champion stupid dunce from coast to coast.

His mother sent him shopping
And told him what to do
She gave him just two nickels
For rice and cabbage, too.
He came back in a hurry

And thus repeated twice
"Which nickel is for cabbage, ma, and which one is for rice?"

Oh, that dumb-bell
That mopey dopey dumb-bell
You never saw a stupid dunce like him.

Unfortunately, Bibo-Lang was not straightforward in their dealings with Ben on "The Bowery Bums," "The Bum's Rush" and "Once a Bum, Always a Bum." The company neither paid accurate royalties nor kept him properly apprised of sheet music sales, and they never even copyrighted the songs (despite the copyright notice at the bottom of the sheet music). That further placed all appropriate financial transactions in jeopardy. Ben eventually sued the firm and settled for $850. The income was most welcome, but it came at the steep price of yet another depressing experience with a music publisher. The deceptions by the New York Melody Company and Bibo-Lang had a deleterious effect on Ben. His faith in the business, already fragile, was more or less shattered by now. Though he may have been an upbeat sort before, he now became, with just a few exceptions, suspicious and distrustful of all music executives, a disposition he found very hard to shake from that point on.

By this time the country had sunk into the Great Depression and, not having a reputation of much worth, it was virtually impossible for Ben to catch another break like the one presented by Velvet-Tone and Bibo-Lang, and the following decade was a dry one for Ben's career as a songwriter. While he didn't stop composing, he began to believe that he'd never amount to anything as a songwriter, and that must have been the most depressing thing of all.

TAKE MY GRANDSON, PLEASE

In the early 1980s I wrote an article for The Staten Island Advance titled "A Life of Laughs, a Legacy of Love," which was about Poppy Benny. I got chastised for it.

By Poppy Benny.

I had just graduated college and was aggressively trying to build up a portfolio of published clips. The article was about how much joy the entertainer Benny Bell had given me through the years, despite being so unsuccessful by all conventional measurements. Only at the very end of the article, in the last line, did I let on that I was talking about my own grandfather.

I felt good about it; not only was I finally published in a daily newspaper, but my article was an affectionate tribute that was given substantial editorial space. I eagerly showed it to Poppy Benny. I wanted him to be as proud of it as I was.

That was a mistake.

Even before I could say hot pants, he warned me—albeit in as gentle a way as he could—that I should never write anything about him in which I admit to a direct relationship. He was scared of the potential consequences.

"What consequences?" I asked.

As it turned out, it was entirely conceivable to him that my sister and I could be kidnapped as a result of any publicity that connected the dots between Benny Bell and the Samberg family name. After all, the song "Shaving Cream," by then, had resurfaced and was very popular, so it wasn't a stretch for anyone, he believed, to assume that Benny Bell was a millionaire.

It bothered me for years afterward. What, I wondered, did that kind of mindset mean in terms of the seriousness of his efforts to be an entertainer? Was he really that scared of success? Is that what held him back? If a scenario like the one he suggested were common, grandchildren of thousands of songwriters and singers and actors and comedians would be kidnapped every day of the year.

Had he somehow become so immodest that he truly believed he had the same level of name recognition as Jack Benny or Henny Youngman or dozens of other famous comedy entertainers? Did he truly have the passion to succeed, or did panic and paranoia render his dreams and goals nothing more than trivial pursuits?

Just what made Poppy Benny tick? Or not tick? I was desperate to know—but at the same time I didn't want to know. The answer might have made me too angry.

In any event, I heeded his warning and refrained from writing anything else about him until after his death. By then, it was quite clear that I wasn't worth kidnapping.

THE GREAT DEPRESSION

Alcoholic fathers, mentally unstable mothers, criminally insane brothers, anorexic sisters and drug addicted spouses are often requirements—or so it seems—for writers to count among their family members in order to be successful. I've had none, which I used to joke (only half-heartedly) was the reason my own success has been so elusive. I have no skeletons in any of my otherwise messy closets.

Then, while going through Ben's papers, I finally had a glimmer of hope. In 1932 he may have come as close to clinical depression as anyone I've ever personally known. A large pamphlet he wrote that year was my clue.

It wasn't alcoholism, but at least it was something.

It would have been easy for Ben to blame his lack of success on the Great Depression that began in 1929. The once booming and effervescent activity of songwriters and song pluggers in New York City's Tin Pan Alley fell victim to economic strife. Several influential music publishers surrendered to the control of motion picture studios that had more money and clout in an industry devoted to what the country sorely needed at that time: fantasy. Quite a number of top songwriters also began working under contract for the movie moguls out west instead of the music moguls back east. Laurence Bergreen, in his biography of Irving Berlin, "As Thousands Cheer," said about the era, "Pedestrians strolled along West 28th Street, once the scene of a flourishing music industry, without hearing so much as a note. If they wondered whatever became of Tin Pan Alley, they would have discovered it had been bought up by Hollywood."

But Ben didn't blame the Depression for his professional woes. He blamed the business itself, mostly, while also reacting to his own inability to write any songs in which publishers, record companies or performers seemed interested.

Still, he kept busy, writing dozens of songs between 1928 and 1935, many of them reflective of the characters that had always fascinated him— songs like "A Hobo's Paradise," "The Crap-Shooting Blues" and "John the Drunkard." To save money, he often copyrighted several songs under one umbrella title, such as "Benny Samberg's Medley of Original Songs," or "Benny Samberg's Second Medley of Original Songs."

He copyrighted two songs in 1929, "Sweet Violets" and "I Bought Some Chewing Gum," both of which gained quite a bit of popularity in the years to follow—but not always with his exact music and lyrics or even his name attached to them.

Ben and Molly had a son, Gerald, on April 11, 1930, born into the kind of tenement poverty glorified and sanitized in the songs Ben wrote during that time period. But it most certainly was not a glorified or sanitized existence for the young family. There was no money. Ben had taken a Notary Public exam a year-and-a-half before, and the few dollars he earned as a notary was often the only income he had. As just one example of their domestic fragility, a month after Jerry was born,

Ben received a letter from a regional coal distributor, Burns Brothers, warning him to pay outstanding bills totaling $154 for coal that had been delivered almost a year earlier.

In October 1930 Ben joined Molly's brother, Nat Ehrlich, as a push-cart peddler in the Williamsburg section of Brooklyn. In October he applied for government relief.

As he had already been doing, Ben continued to enter amateur contests both as a sketch comic and a singer. Entrants lucky enough to win events such as Loew's Comic Contest or J.C. Flippen's Amateur Contest (both of which Ben entered—the latter under the stage name Benny Goodman) could walk away with prize money and, more importantly, visibility and recognition.

Ben fared well in several of the contests, but didn't actually win any of them.

Then, the following year, he wrote a 20-page discourse which he called "The Complete Catalog of Original Songs Written and Composed by Benny Samberg," although that is far from a complete and accurate description of its content. It was actually a manifesto railing against music publishers, while also calling into serious question his own talent. Full of anger and gloom, the entire 1700-word opening is an almost lyrical treatise on the state of the songwriting business at the time.

"Broadway," he wrote, "covers a multitude of heartaches. Few and fortunate are those who escape the hazards of its ugly discrimination. I doubt that I will ever forget or forgive the misery and discomfort it brought me in the past. Try as I may, I find it impossible not to feel in my heart the horrible discouragement to which I was subjected in my frantic effort to gain prominence as a professional songwriter. How those publishers laughed at me! How they kidded me and gave me the most unpardonable runabouts; but I was a glutton for punishment and embodied all their ridicule and mistreatment for years and years.... Many are the times that I mailed them a manuscript, only to have it returned UNOPENED! Just think of it, rejecting a contribution without a fair evaluation."

But in almost the same breath he willingly holds himself partially accountable: "Their antagonism will never be dispelled from my mind, although sometimes I can hardly blame them, for when I review the songs which I frequently submitted for their approval, I am obliged to emit a giggle at the inferior quality of many of these musical compositions.... Yet," he is quick to add, "this should not vindicate those music publishers who made my life miserable, because they even treated GOOD amateurs in just the same rotten manner."

The book also includes an alphabetical listing of the 270 songs he had written up to that point, and a reprint of a 'memorandum of agreement' between a publishing company and a songwriter—not the kind of agreement he ever signed as a songwriter, but the kind he would have *liked* to have signed, had publishing companies been decent enough to write them the way he suggested.

Finally, there is a warning to anyone who might come across the book in an underhanded way: "If it so happens that this book is stolen together with any other household articles, you may keep all valuables in your possession but PLEASE be human enough to send back this book. All the years of hard labor in the making of it is melted into this book and to destroy it would be as much of a crime as murder. The author promises you on his word of honor that positively NO arrest will be made and not one word will be mentioned to anybody. You do not have to deliver it personally if you don't want to; you may send it by parcel post or express, but for God's sake, DON'T DESTROY IT, PLEASE! Once more, I swear to you sacredly that not a single word will be said to any living soul and the author hopes that you will be decent enough to see that it gets back to him somehow. All your other vices will practically be eradicated by the virtue of this good deed."

The manuscript, written when he was just 25 years old, is torturous, emotional, confused, anxious and eccentric.

Just like him.

Somebody Ought to do a Tribute

*I*n October 2004, through the efforts of my friend Bill Freytag, a record collector, I became acquainted with Brian Gari, whose grandfather was an old-time comic slightly more famous than mine—Eddie Cantor. Brian was involved with an organization called Friends of Old-Time Radio and was helping to plan its 29th annual convention at a hotel near Newark Liberty International Airport. After a few conversations with Brian, during which I brought him up to date on the late Benny Bell's career and family, he decided to ask my father to sit on a 'Singers and Musicians Panel' that he was hosting during the convention.

It didn't matter to Brian that the showbiz legacy of Benny Bell paled by comparison to his own grandfather's, or that others on the panel were more accomplished old-time singers and performers, such as Jill Corey, Louise O'Brien and Jane Kean. To Brian, having the oldest son of that nutty, crazy, singular novelty sensation named Benny Bell (whose work he knew well) was perfectly acceptable for his panel. My father agreed to do it. My mother accompanied him to the convention. I was there, as well.

It was a terrific evening. First, I saw Joe Franklin in the lobby of the hotel and went over to talk to him. After introducing myself and chatting a little bit about my grandfather, Franklin smiled and said,

"He was something else, that guy. Somebody ought to do a tribute. A show or something. It's long overdue."

I wanted to suggest that he be the one to do it, but by then Franklin was 78 years old, had no television show of his own and only very limited exposure on the radio. Still, it was pleasing to hear him say it.

Then, during the 'Singers and Musicians Panel,' my father's speech was very warmly received; he did a superb job telling a few relevant stories and answering a few pertinent questions about the life and times of Benny Bell, and when he was finished, Brian Gari played a tape of the Benny Bell song, "Everybody Wants My Fanny," and the laughter in the room was rowdy, genuine and infectious:

Everyone is out to get my Fanny
Everybody wants to see my Fanny
Everybody likes to hold my Fanny
But she loves no one but me

Everybody wants to seize my Fanny
Everybody likes to squeeze my Fanny
They do everything to please my Fanny
Still she loves no one but me

Oh, don't touch my Fanny
Please don't ever try
My little Fanny
Is reserved for just one guy

That's why I'll never let another love light blind me
Everywhere I go you'll always find me
With my little Fanny right behind me
'Cause she's so in love with me

We will be married

Some day next June

And when we go away

To spend our honeymoon

I know that everyone is gonna miss my Fanny

No one ever could resist my Fanny

But they wouldn't dare to kiss my Fanny

'Cause she's so in love with me.

The recording had been re-mastered in 1975 and it sounded as if Benny Bell, with his voice loud and clear, was in the packed room along with the rest of the crowd, making us all smile and laugh with sweet abandon. It was quite a wonderful thing to behold. It was, in one respect, the tribute that Joe Franklin had suggested—although limited in scope and attendance. No matter what the final verdict of his career may be, that night in the fall of 2004 Benny Bell was one of the biggest stars in comedy heaven. A giant. A legend. And in some ways I was never as proud to be the grandson of Benny Bell as I was at the Newark Holiday Inn that night, when he was singing about his Fanny.

Sour Pickles

There were more missed opportunities than mysteries in Ben's songwriting career. But there were indeed a few mysteries. It's not hard to fantasize—though quite hard to believe—that he engineered some of the mysteries as a way to give himself a much-needed promotional boost. After all, any publicity is good publicity, as long as it doesn't land you in jail.

Ben had gotten into scrapes, but he never landed in jail.

Those who knew him knew he wasn't a contentious man. Paranoid and distrustful, yes, but he never actively looked for trouble and would much rather have signed copyright forms than depositions. But the music business is one that is fraught with many stumbling blocks of contention, planned or otherwise. An inspiration can turn out to have already inspired someone else years earlier, and a combination of notes can bear a striking resemblance to someone else's much older combination of notes. Even the great Irving Berlin had his share of lawsuits by people claiming he plagiarized their songs.

"Sweet Violets" is one of those mysteries that skirted the issue of plagiarism. It has been an extremely popular double-entendre party song since 1922, when Ben first copyrighted it. In fact, there are some who say it was extremely popular years *before* he copyrighted it, which is, of course, an important part of the mystery.

As Ben told the story in an article he wrote for *Melody Lane* magazine shortly after the song was published, when he was 16 years old he was walking on the beach in Coney Island when he heard a bunch of kids singing a rowdy round of verses, using a common, beer-hall waltz arrangement (he called it a "gang-song"). The lyrics left obscenity to the imagination because of the way the potentially dirty words were replaced at the last moment with non-objectionable ones.

"I was very much impressed—in fact, amused by the basic idea of such a novel ditty," Ben wrote, "and without a moment's hesitation I promptly agreed with myself that it would be extraordinary for me to write something legitimate along those lines... I do not recall whether somebody passed by with a bouquet of flowers which prompted me to choose 'Sweet Violets' for the title and the distracting substitute—I might have chosen 'Raw Onions' or 'Sour Pickles' to serve the purpose, but for some unknown reason as good as any other, I picked 'Sweet Violets' and the name stuck."

> *When I was a handsome young fellow*
> *I sure had the time of my life*
> *But one day a man broke my backbone*
> *When I ran away with his...*
>
> *Sweet violets, sweeter than all the roses*
> *Covered all over from head to foot*
> *Covered all over with snow.*
>
> *One day I forgot my suspenders*
> *And took my girl out to a dance*

While dancing I heard someone holler
"Hey mister, you're losing your...

Sweet violets, sweeter than all the roses
Covered all over from head to foot
Covered all over with snow.

At one point in the mid 1920s he sang the song at a boys' camp in New Jersey where he had been hired to perform, and as the story goes, the reaction was quite spectacular. The campers ate it up and begged him for the lyrics. Ben claims it was from that one event at the camp that the song started to spread. Before long, he got reports of people singing it as far away as California. Meanwhile, the song also began to evolve into "a vulgar creature," in his words, "with its respectable verses replaced by some of the most distorted, filthy and obscene lyrics that I ever heard in all my life."

Publishers up and down Tin Pan Alley rejected "Sweet Violets," perhaps because of the ill repute it now had with its alternate set of obscene lyrics. It wasn't until late in 1928 that Ben realized the value of having it copyrighted with his own lyrics intact, to minimize some of negative reactions from publishers and as a way of getting the original heard. He received the copyright certificate in January 1929. Then, another roadblock: a publisher told him that he had heard the song before, with the same title and the same chorus, which could lead to significant legal problems.

In the *Melody Lane* article Ben describes how inadvertent plagiarism—and sometimes even conscious borrowing—is a common occurrence in songwriting. Both Ben in his 1932 article and Laurence Bergreen in his 1990 biography of Irving Berlin cite the song "Yes, We Have No Bananas" as having been built from bits and pieces of at least five other songs. In the case of "Sweet Violets," the 'borrowing' was done from what Ben believed was an ancient public domain "gang-song." But what he didn't know when he copyrighted it was that it was still copyrighted by the prestigious publisher, Theodore Presser.

So Ben immediately sent "Sweet Violets" to the Theodore Presser Company and, according to his article, "They returned the manuscript with a most courteous reply to the effect that they see no similarity between my song and the one which they published many years ago under the same title."

With that potential problem eliminated, he was able to sign with the Southern Music Company in May 1932 to publish "Sweet Violets," and before long it was snatched up by several recording artists, including Beatrice Lillie, the trio Anne, Judy and Zeke (Judy was comedienne Judy Canova), and The Eton Boys, who had recorded with Cliff Edwards and also supplied music for many of the Betty Boop cartoons. There were at least eight recorded versions in the 1930s, by as many artists on as many labels (including Decca, Oriole and Vocalion), and the song became a staple at countless parties and performances. Ben recorded it, too, several times, one of which was a lively, stylish, highly jazzed version featuring harmonizing trumpets and background vocals.

It was still popular in 1951 when Bob Hope and Bing Crosby did a take-off on it (which in essence was a novelty version of a novelty song) during an armed services radio broadcast. That was the same year that Dinah Shore recorded her own version, which was credited not to Ben, but to Cy Coben and Charles Grean who, like Ben, probably assumed they were merely adapting an old public domain song. It seemed to have been around in so many versions for so many decades that to write it anew was a perfectly reasonable objective. In the Dinah Shore adaptation, all that remained of Ben's copyrighted version was the chorus—and even that was altered slightly.

Ben claims to have come up with the title on his own, and that the music was reminiscent but not identical to the earlier tune. However, the first four measures of the song that started it all tell a slightly different story. The original "Sweet Violets" was composed by Joseph Emit in 1882 for his play, "Fritz Among the Gypsies," and the two key words in the introduction to the chorus of Emmett's song are sung with the exact notes, and in the exact time signature, as in the song Ben wrote 40 years later. The rest of it *is* different—but the key phrase, "Sweet Violets," is identical in words and music.

It is highly unlikely that Ben knowingly misrepresented himself when he recounted the birth of his own "Sweet Violets." He was always a generous man, quite willing to share credit where it should rightly be shared. In 1946, for example, he gave several hundred dollars to a friend who had suggested he turn his "Pincus the Peddler" persona into a song (which eventually sold very well), and in 1956 he signed an agreement giving co-authorship credit and royalties to another friend who had simply suggested the title and basic theme for a song called "Indian Rock n' Roll," which Ben subsequently recorded. He would not have assumed that he conceived the phrase "Sweet Violets" unless he really believed it.

So did my grandfather write one of the most famous wordplay novelty songs of all time? Not exactly. But he helped popularize it, provided a good property for half a dozen singers, and made a pretty damn good recording of the song himself. And he probably should have gotten more credit for it.

THE KID WITH THE DRUM

My grandfather always called me *The Kid with the Drum*. I'm not sure why. I never played the drums.

Maybe he had problems getting good drummers over the years and wanted to groom me for the time when we might record together.

Maybe it was simply because I tapped a lot. Banging out the solo from the song "Wipe Out" on the kitchen table was a ritual for all young American males in the 1960s who wanted to prove they could be rock stars. Perhaps he saw me do it one too many times.

Or maybe it was because someone gave him old drum equipment, which presented him with a cost-effective opportunity to give me a present he knew no one else would ever give me. The Kid with the Drum moniker may have just been a convenient way of letting my parents know that there was no way in hell he would be taking the stuff back home with him. Heaven knows there was no room in his apartment for anything new—at least nothing bigger than a harmonica. His place was already packed corner to corner with reel-to-reel tape recorders, microphones, albums, stationery supplies, magazines and who knows what else. One of the 'peddler songs' that shows up on a few of his latter-day comedy albums was called "You Name It, I Got It," and anyone visiting his apartment would understand instantly where he got the idea.

Anyway, the drum collection he gave me started with a snare. A few months later came a bass. And finally he brought over a huge black trunk with big rusted silver latches. It was one of those sturdy old trunks like the ones vaudevillians used to tote around with them to carry all their props and costumes. Maybe it had been.

Inside were drum sticks, brushes, mallets, a woodblock, a cowbell, cymbals, a high-hat stand, a pedal for the bass drum and various other percussion paraphernalia. All of it ancient and authentic. A drummer's paradise.

But I didn't play the drums.

That hardly mattered—neither to him nor me. I loved the trunk because it was my daily connection to Poppy Benny, and he loved it because he got to call me The Kid with the Drum.

That trunk stayed in my parents' basement throughout my college years and while I moved from one apartment to another, first as a young trade magazine editor and then as a newlywed. Finally, when my wife Bonnie and I moved into our first house, the trunk came with us, and then into our second. Somewhere along the line, it became part of a garage sale, with most of the accessories still inside. After all, my mother had made fun of Poppy Benny's apartment all the time I was growing up—the way he saved countless bits and pieces of this and that and the other thing—and I learned to regard it as an undesirable trait. Besides, Bonnie and I were probably overwhelmed with the amount of stuff we had collected over the previous ten years and simply thought it was a good idea to get rid of it.

Now, I'm overwhelmed with my stupidity in letting it go.

CHIDDA BIDDA BIM BUM

Oh, to have been a fly on the wall in that apartment...

On November 16, 1936 Ben had a meeting in Manhattan that could have—and *should* have—lifted his career to an entirely new level.

Just four years after writing the angry "Complete Catalog" document, Ben met a man named Lou Levy in the offices of Words and Music, Inc., a major publisher in New York City. Ben was there to push his latest ditty, "I Know a Crazy Song," which was, in essence, simply a crazy song—one that cleverly promoted itself through the repetition of its nonsensical chorus: "Yodda wee-hee wah-ha, chidda-bidda bim-bum boo..."

Words and Music, Inc. did indeed publish "I Know a Crazy Song," but Levy was impressed enough with the 30-year-old songwriter's quirky personality to invite him over to his own apartment the following day for further discussions. Levy also had his own publishing and promotions company, Leeds Music, which he had co-founded with two other young songwriters he had discovered, Sammy Cahn and Saul Chaplin, both of whom, it turned out, were at Levy's apartment the day Ben was invited to stop by.

A fourth gentleman, Dave Kapp, was also there. He, too, was a promoter and record company executive.

(According to Ben, while he was talking with Levy and Kapp in the apartment, Cahn and Chaplin were by the piano writing lyrics to "Bie Mir Bist du Shoen," which soon became a major hit for the Andrews Sisters.)

Based on their accomplishments up to that point alone, Levy and Kapp would have been exceptional people for Ben to have in his corner. And had Ben been able to somehow analyze those accomplishments and predict where those gentlemen might be headed, he may have recognized the need to do whatever was necessary to get them solidly in his corner. Levy, as it turned out, went on to help build the careers of Henry Mancini, Petula Clark, Bobby Darin and Bob Dylan, and published the Beatles' first American hit, "I Want to Hold Your Hand." And Kapp's work for Brunswick and Decca Records were highlighted by his contributions to the careers of the Andrews Sisters, the Ink Spots and Roger Williams, among others.

The specific conversation that was held in Lou Levy's apartment that day in the winter of '36 is lost to time. But because of Ben's past experiences with publishers, his disappointment in the methods and practices of many people in the business, and what is known to have been his general frame of mind (by virtue of what he wrote in the "Complete Catalog" manifesto), it is entirely conceivable that he displayed an attitude that was somewhat less than gracious, and probably made requests, perhaps even demands, that met with little interest from either Levy or Kapp.

He may have written a crazy song, but Levy and Kapp probably thought the guy was just crazy.

BORSCHT AND FOUND

It took him 76 years to venture any further west than the west side of Manhattan. In my grandfather's mind, the center of the universe was in New York City; he'd be lost anywhere else.

Even when he was relatively comfortable in our Westbury home during Sunday visits, it was a poor substitute for home; somehow it was always clear that Westbury wasn't Brooklyn. Case closed.

My mother's father, Dave Mogel, seemed much more at home during his visits to our house from his own apartment nearby in Floral Park. Poppy Dave would stand by the front door and look out at the lawn and the sidewalk and the kids playing on the other side of the street, or he'd go into my father's workroom in the basement and tinker around, or he'd shuffle down the hallway by the kitchen and look at all the pictures on the walls. Not Poppy Benny. He would sit in the same chair all afternoon and sing and hum within the special world he brought with him wherever he went. He was perfectly friendly, and always amusing—but his heart and mind were obviously closer to the Brooklyn Bridge than the Long Island Expressway. I didn't mind; he always told me funny stories, sang crazy songs and taught me how to play them. Not only that, but since I had always expressed a certain interest in the entertainment world (and also because I was the only grandson), I was clearly the heir apparent—not in my parents' eyes, but in my own.

Other than New York City, there was one other place where Poppy Benny was at ease and well suited: the Catskill Mountains. He never seemed lost there. It was more of a home away from home than anywhere else beyond the Hudson River. Poppy Benny and Grandma Molly went to the mountains several times while their family was growing, and when my sister and I were young the tradition continued. He performed there sporadically throughout the years, singing both his Yiddish and English novelty songs. The settings were never those associated with many of the Borscht Belt legends—places like Grossinger's, the Browns', the Concord, Kutscher's, the Pines or the Tamarack Lodge, where the likes of Jerry Lewis, Danny Kaye, Milton Berle, The Ritz Brothers, Jack Carter and Buddy Hackett could often be found performing; they were smaller, less famous places with names like Saperstein's Farm, Rubinstein's Hotel, and the Evans Kiamesha Hotel. Still, they were bona fide Borscht Belt destinations, and Poppy Benny was actually on many of their bills, if never on any of their billboards.

I liked my Catskill getaways very much, not just because of the relaxation and fresh mountain air, but also because my grandfather had an air of celebrity about him wherever he performed. I felt very special in my role as the heir apparent.

There were several mountain trips for me over the years—sometimes with my parents and sister, sometimes with one set of grandparents, sometimes with the other, and sometimes with both. Every Catskill summer was a special summer.

I'd swim, read a book on a big Adirondack chair, and watch the occasional Benny Bell performance. I remember seeing him from time to time talking to an emcee or a bandleader, and I knew that he had somehow become Catskill royalty over the years, even though there were never any placards at the clubhouse entrances with his picture, as there were of other performers. I was too young, and uninformed, to make heads or tails of the unusual career track that made him what he was. I didn't know those other performers all had agents and managers (and at least a little bit of trust to go along with it). But it hardly mattered to me at the time.

There's one rather disconcerting memory I have, however, involving a stay at the Evans Hotel in Kiamesha Lake. I was nine years old. We had stayed at the Evans several times. Poppy Benny was talking to the house bandleader, Vic Carlton, on the lawn outside the clubhouse, and I was off to the side, waiting for him. Apparently Carlton was saying something about me. Carlton then turned to me and asked if I wanted to perform that night in the clubhouse, along with my grandfather. Being very shy—and taken completely by surprise—I said no. Poppy Benny whispered something to Carlton, presumably both to close the topic and save me from any embarrassment, and that was that.

In the months and years that followed I realized I had never been as disappointed in myself as I was that afternoon. While I had no desire to become a professional singer, I did get a charge, and a confidence boost, whenever I sang and played the guitar in front of a small gathering of relatives and friends. Performing that night at the Evans may not have changed the direction of my life, but it could have been a nice little memory to look back on with pride, and may have even been an important mile marker to revisit whenever I needed a lift for the future. What did I have to lose, anyway? It would have been fun. Poppy Benny would never have said no. It was not in him to pass up an invitation like that. But I did. Some heir! My parents had no reason to worry: I'd never be a Benny Bell.

Go to Work, You Jerk

After the meeting in Lou Levy's apartment in 1936, which resulted in no joint projects or partnerships, Ben decided to take matters into his own hands, apparently having drawn the conclusion that doing so was the only way to build a career in the music business. No one else, he believed, would have his best interests at heart. No one else would treat him with the honesty, principles and ethics that he felt he (and others like him) deserved. He knew it would be hard work, but he'd rather grow weary from that than from dealing with people who were worth a lot less than the fancy desks they sat behind.

In June 1937 he became friendly with an executive at RCA Records named Eli Oberstein, who suggested that he concentrate his efforts on making records for the coin-operated machine market, soon to be more popularly known as jukeboxes. The machines were located at hundreds of thousands of bars, saloons and soda shops across the country, where the patrons were more or less in charge of what was played in them over and over and over again (which, depending on popularity, could lead to many consumer sales). So Ben began to write risqué songs specifically for the jukebox trade. Using a friend as his vocalist, he recorded several songs at a studio on West 48th Street in Manhattan, but didn't like the way the recordings came out. So he rerecorded them, singing the songs himself, though he listed himself on the records as Al Driggs. (The friend he had previously used was also named Al.) Once again, he was dissatisfied with the results, primarily because there was a loud buzz on the recordings. Having made a deal with a small, obscure record label called Arrow, Ben was able to sell 200 discs to a major jukebox vending company, but didn't earn nearly as much money doing so as he spent putting the project together. Apparently, the rational for using the pseudonym was to keep the records as untraceable as possible, since they included such titles as "That Dog-Gone Window, I Can't Get it Up Any More," "Johnny's Little Horse" and "Nice Little Pussy." Ben wanted to sew his novelty seeds cautiously. He did not want to get in trouble.

Ben continued to write songs—62 of them between 1937 and 1944—and decided to continue producing and recording them himself. But even a solo effort such as the one he was now attempting as a songwriter-singer-producer required a publishing company and a record label to open doors and maintain some semblance of legitimacy, if only for the sake of keeping legal accounts of income. Back in 1929 he had taken a cue from Irving Berlin and Harry Von Tilzer by starting a little company of his own, Monarch Publishing, to publish his songs. Two years later he founded its sister company, Monarch Music, to produce the records. There had been little action from either concern. Now, in 1937, he was ready to try again with two new ventures, the Novelty Song Company to handle the publishing and the Radio Novelty Records Company to handle production. (Throughout the years he would also use Cocktail, Embassy, Enterprise, Hudson, Popular Songwriting, and Zion as the names of his own music companies.)

As far as the songs were concerned, while colorful derelicts continued to appear in such compositions as "Go to Work, You Jerk," "Horses Work, Not Me," "I Had but Fifty Cents," "Dopey John" and "Dopey Joe," Ben stuck to the wordplay and double entendres with which he had already begun experimenting. "Snow Balls" and "Nobody Ever Died from It" were among the first of these. Some of the new songs did indeed catch on in the jukebox market, as he had hoped—though usually not right away. Some of them made fun of women while blessing their attributes, others made fun of idle worship, and still others, like "My Janitor's Can," lectured on the good and evil of childlike behavior:

> *I don't care if you play on the sidewalk*
> *I don't mind if you dance in the hall*
> *You can even play ball on the staircase*
> *Or with chalk scratch your name on the wall.*
>
> *I don't care if you ransack the basement*
> *If you're happy, then I'm happy too*
> *But don't stick a burning cigar in my can*
> *That's all that I ask of you.*
>
> *I don't care if you smash out a window*
> *I don't mind if you slide down the rail*
> *I don't care if you play with my pussy*
> *Just as long as you don't pull its tail.*
>
> *I don't care if you pull off the molding*
> *I'll forgive anything that you do*
> *But don't stick a burning cigar in my can*
> *That's all that I ask of you.*

Around this time he also started buying recording equipment, instruments, and even tools and machinery to do his own printing, in essence building his very own soup-to-nuts musical conglomerate right there in the basement of his apartment building on Elton Street, in the East New York section of Brooklyn. By 1946 the operation included a Rek-O-Cut master cutter with which he was able to produce vinyl discs. He would then bring the master discs elsewhere to be produced in quantity.

Still, his meager income from record and sheet music sales (and a few lingering royalty checks from the old days) had to be supplemented, so he took several trivial jobs now and then, such as delivering phone books, doing light clerical duties or working as a busboy. He was also forced to apply for governmental aid once more; in February 1938 he received $17 a week for several weeks, and another $5 from the Jewish Aid Society.

It was during these lean years that some of the gentlemen with whom Ben had met from time to time began reaching tremendous heights in the business. Ted Collins from the Velvet Tone Record Company had become vice president of Columbia Records, as well as Kate Smith's manager. In 1938 Collins acquired Irving Berlin's "God Bless America" for Smith, turning it into an unofficial national anthem. Sammy Cahn, now partnering with Jule Styne, was writing scores for successful movies such as "Anchors Away" and "The Kid from Brooklyn." Frank Luther, who had recorded "Oh, That Dumb-Bell," was getting very popular and would soon receive his own star on the Hollywood Walk of Fame.

And while Ted Collins, Sammy Cahn and Frank Luther were busy shooting their stars ever faster and higher into the musical stratosphere, Ben was busy looking for a way to make "My Janitor's Can" the next big jukebox hit in New York.

KOSHER COMEDY

A few years ago I wrote a play called "Assorted Nuts at Passover, or, The Night I Felt Like I Became the Last Real Jew Left in America," and it wouldn't take a genius to guess that the apartment in which the play takes place is modeled on the one Grandma Molly and Poppy Benny lived in on East 16th Street, in the Sheepshead Bay section of Brooklyn, and that the characters of Sam and Miriam Lasher are based on Ben and Molly Samberg.

The apartment described in the play is small—a kitchen, a living room (which doubles as a dining room), a bedroom and a bathroom. The story takes place on three seder nights during Passover, in three consecutive years. An extended family of parents, siblings, aunts, uncles and cousins are present in each of the three acts, stuffed like picked herrings into the living room, which takes up the entire stage. At one point, in one of the acts, a character comes out of the bathroom with a quizzical look on her face and announces,

"There's a huge tape recorder in the bathtub!"

I didn't make that part up.

Had an outsider visited the real-life East 16th Street seders he might walk away with the impression that they weren't particularly religious affairs. But he wouldn't be right. Poppy Benny handled the religious part almost all by himself. Over the years it had developed into a routine: he would say the prayers and perform the rituals on everyone's behalf, while the rest of the family talked, argued and kvetched before the meal was served. The funny part was that even my grandfather talked, argued and kvetched while he was conducting the service.

He'd be at the head of the table reading, in a quiet chant, the Passover haggadah, which is the little book that families use to recount the story of Exodus. But he'd also hear what the rest of us were talking about and would sometimes stop his chanting to join in and offer a comment or two. Occasionally it would turn into an extended anecdote or opinion, and someone would always have to yell at him to continue. "Ben, read!" "Read, Uncle Benny! Read." "Terrific, pop—now read!"

So then he'd return to the book. Moments later he'd look up again and tell another story. "Benny, read!" someone would command. So he'd bury his face in the haggadah for a while, only to then try to top someone's anecdote with one of his own. That's when Grandma Molly would yell from the kitchen, where she was putting the finishing touches on the meal, "Stop it already, Benny! Just read!"

Then he'd conclude with a prayer and a song, and we'd eat.

There was always quite a crowd—my parents and my sister Irene, my Uncle Charley and my cousins Debbie and Laurie, Poppy Benny's brother Sidney and his wife Sally, and often another two or three relatives—each one a character in a real-life play.

Everyone was more than sufficiently aware of just how much stuff there was in the apartment. In fact, sometimes we had to vie with the stuff in order to have a place to sit.

Some of the stuff—not always the big stuff, but the smaller stuff, instead—provided amusing little diversions during the seders. Like the discovery *of one of those little picture trees with the hanging circles that people keep on dressers with family photos placed in each of the circles. Nothing too unusual about that—other than the fact that the one Poppy Benny had still had the pictures that came with the tree when it was purchased ten or eleven years before. Or the little wrapped sugary candies called Violets that were in ashtrays and dishes all over the apartment, and which nobody but my grandfather ever seemed to eat.*

Of course, with a ukulele, several harmonicas, pitch pipes and other tuneful paraphernalia strewn about, the story of Moses often shared equal time with the sound of music.

But despite the interruptions, the East 16th Street seders were complete seders, with the gifilte fish and the horseradish and the dipping of the wine and the washing of the hands and the hiding of the matzo, and there was always an underlying sense of dignity and delight that went along with it. And that's because my grandfather, the son of a part-time cantor, was a full-time Jew, with all attendant joy and pride that goes along with it. Conversations at these seders were rarely too serious, or too political, or even too religious, but there were occasions when Poppy Benny would be incited to get emotional about something or other, and chances were that it had something to do with Judaism. He was a supporter of Israel; he worried that too much intermarriage would shrink an already dwindling Jewish population; he reveled in the accomplishments of Jewish movers and shakers and politicians (and, of course, performers).

That joy and pride shone through, too, in the Jewish and Yiddish work with which he was involved through the years. Between 1944 and 1962 he recorded and released several dozen Jewish and Yiddish songs, many of which found a small but loyal audience in many of New York City's Jewish communities. To me, those were the songs on which he sang with all his heart and soul, more so than on any of his other work. He recorded a few ceremonial albums for Jewish occasions, such as "Benny Bell Blesses the Bride" (with a photo of my father, Poppy Benny and Poppy Dave on the cover), which had an air of passion and purpose to it that his novelty work did not always achieve. He had other albums with songs for bar mitzvahs and other events. In the notebooks and ledgers in which he listed his Yiddish and Hebrew compositions, he wrote their titles in both English and in Hebrew, and the handwritten Hebrew lettering was always robust and perfect, as if making a statement that this was the language he loved the most. He wrote several freylachs, which were joyful instrumental dance tunes. One of them, "The Benny Bell Freylach," achieved quite a measure of popularity and success among the Jewish communities of New York City. The tunes were musically accomplished and memorable, with devotion and zeal in every note. Beginning in the late 1930s many of these recordings were broadcast on some of the Yiddish-language radio stations that were on the air at the time. (There were more than a dozen in New York alone.)

He even made a record called "Hebrew Lessons" which was precisely that—an elementary Hebrew lesson. It probably held no marketing promise at all, but it sounded as if he were in his element doing it.

Of course, he also wrote and recorded quite a number of Jewish and Yiddish novelty songs in albums such as "Kosher Comedy" and "Kosher Twist."

In 1950, eight years before Irving Berlin wrote his own Zionist tribute, Poppy Benny composed a song for the independence of the Jewish State, called "Home Again in Israel," that is palpable in its emotion and sincerity, and an extremely accomplished musical composition:

> Home again in Israel
> At last no more need I roam

My sacred land, oh beautiful Israel
You are now my home sweet home.

For years and years they broke our homes
We had no place to hide
They crushed our souls, they lashed us
But our spirit never died
We dreamed about a homeland that would banish all such fear
And now at last it's here
Shema Yisrael

Home again in Israel
Our dream of dreams has come true
My shining star, oh beautiful Israel
I am coming back to you.

He enjoyed his Jewish and Yiddish work. He felt drawn to it. But it was a genre of songwriting on which he never really concentrated with the energy he reserved for his other material. I'm convinced he should have. His dream of dreams may have come true.

Take a Ship

One of Ben's little marketing gimmicks in the 1960s was a "Certificate of Sanity," which he tried to sell to consumers who thought that other people considered them insane. It wouldn't surprise me if the idea sprung from the three-year period between 1937 and 1940 when he nearly *did* go insane trying to sell his records. It was a series of events that might have driven other people completely over the edge.

It all began shortly after Eli Oberstein planted the idea in his head to distribute novelty tunes to the jukebox trade. In May 1937 Ben recorded two songs, "Sweet Violets" and "Hootshe Kootshe," at a studio in midtown Manhattan, ordered labels at a print shop downtown, and pressed 200 discs at a plant across the Hudson River in Newark, New Jersey. The problems began almost immediately.

The first predicament had to do with the record labels. They were printed in very light gold letters on a reflective back background, making the words barely legible. That would render word of mouth publicity almost impossible: how you can tell someone to buy a certain record if you don't know what the record is called or who recorded it?

Things got worse from there. Once the records were distributed to jukebox operators it was discovered that the groove on the discs was incorrectly pressed and did not allow the auto-return arms on the jukeboxes to work properly.

All 200 discs were useless.

Later that month, in addition to a new version of "Sweet Violets," Ben recorded three more songs, "Horses Work, Not Me," "She's Still Got It" (using the Club Cassada Orchestra, to which he paid a total of $30), and "Once a Bum, Always a Bum," which had already been recorded by Hobo Jack Turner nine years earlier. The songs were published by his own Novelty Song Company and the records produced by his own Radio Novelty Records Corporation. A representative from American Record Corporation (ARC) approached Ben and talked him into pressing the plates there, because they could do it cheaper and wouldn't make the same mistake that the Newark plant had made.

Ben ordered an initial pressing of 1200 discs, but the first set of records that ARC pressed did, in fact, have the same groove problem as the earlier batch and had to be re-pressed. Meanwhile, he began approaching jukebox operators with samples, and many of the operators were interested in the tunes and asked to be put on the list to receive the records once they were made. Unfortunately, it took so many weeks for the records to be pressed that several of the operators cancelled their orders before the records arrived. Ben was apoplectic.

During this time he talked to financiers and even advertised for partners to help fund the solo novelty venture, but no one was interested. So he continued on alone, finally delivered the records—and before long the idea began to show some promise. Based on jukebox play and publicity, by October he sold approximately 2500 records, at 25¢ each.

The sudden activity primed him to be a bit more daring in his choice of song, which was probably what Oberstein had in mind in the first place. Ben worked diligently on almost a dozen raunchy tunes, orchestrating them, hiring the bands and recording them himself. Then he went back to ARC. He still owed them money from the first pressing and paid them as much as he could, with the promise to come through with the rest as soon as possible.

ARC pressed 1000 records, and Ben hit the roof when he discovered that the grooves on the new discs were so small that jukebox and record player tone arms jumped and never played the records all the way through.

"This forced me out of business, and the Novelty Song Company came to an abrupt end," he lamented in one of his journals.

As if all this weren't enough, another company with a name similar to his, Novelty Record Distributing Company, suddenly found itself under investigation by federal authorities for the raunchy recordings it was distributing. That scared Ben, and he made a decision to stick to 'naughty' rather than 'raunchy' songs. In fact, he declined to even list the ones he made with ARC in his notes and journals, perhaps as a way of hiding any evidence that could one day get him into trouble with the authorities.

Trouble found him anyway. In March 1938 he was served a summons by ARC for the money he still owed them for the original pressings. He counter claimed that the merchandise was defective. A court date was set. After meeting with the Legal Aid Society for suggestions, Ben represented himself in court and lost the case. (He offered the company royalties on some of his current songs, a proposal that ARC roundly refused.) A receiver was appointed by the court to sell Ben's copyrights at public auction, but Ben scrounged up $10 to show evidence of good faith, and was given ten days to come up with the rest of the judgment.

"I have no idea where I'll get the money. I am very harassed and troubled," he wrote at the time.

While all this was happening, he continued to write and record novelty songs, and run around from studios to printers to pressing plants to jukebox operators throughout New York, New Jersey and Connecticut to manufacture and then market them. This time he added a new element to the mix: he printed advertising cards for some of the records and sent them to as many jukebox operators as he could find in an effort to create a buzz for the songs. The one he wrote for "I'll Never Get Drunk Again," which he recorded as Benny Bimbo, said:

> This is the new "Novelty" record. A clean, legitimate, respectable number with a bunch of silly noises. It may give you a very good play. Try a few on your machines. Price 45¢ each. (45¢ may be a lot of money for a record when you buy many dozens weekly, but when you try out 6 or so, what does it matter? Believe me, it costs ME more. You see, we're in business for the love of it. Anyway, give us a break.)

As much as it was an advertising pitch, it was also a desperate plea.

Some of the funds he needed to hire bands, print labels, press records and produce ad fliers came from a cousin through marriage, Sadie Keshlonsky, who was also a neighbor. Sadie loaned him money over the next two years and didn't seem to mind how slowly he paid it back. He sold only about 175 copies of "I'll Never Get Drunk Again." Two newer songs, "Hey Joe, Two Beers" and "I Had but Fifty Cents," also had disappointing sales. He was ready to give up.

But in May 1939 he decided to give it one last shot. He wrote a song called "Take a Ship for Yourself," adopted the name Benny Bell, and went to work.

"If this one doesn't come out good," he wrote, "I am through with records."

Using an eight-piece band led by a musician named Frankie 'Miggs' Rand, Ben recorded the song and pressed 200 discs. But within a few weeks, less than 20 records had been sold. Ben was convinced that the companies he had to deal with—the studios, the disc pressers, the jukebox operators—were refusing to work with him. But why? Was it his poor track record, the recent lawsuit brought on by ARC, the titles of his songs? Was he just too much trouble to deal with? He was certain that he was being blacklisted and that there wasn't much he could do about it.

Then, beginning on July 10, 1939, a little more than a month after accepting delivery of 200 records, Ben began receiving dozens of orders for "Take a Ship for Yourself." Apparently the few he had already sold were being played repeatedly and prompting word-of-mouth excitement across the city. Suddenly there was a huge demand for what became to be referred to (more innocuously) as "The Boat Song." But there was one serious problem: he didn't have enough records to fill the orders.

Ben needed to have the records pressed, and fast. He approached one company after another—Decca, Columbia, United States Record Company—but either he was turned down or the prices they demanded were too prohibitive.

On July 20 he was still receiving orders for "The Boat Song" from retailers all over the city—300 from the Bloomfield Record Store, 100 from the Sultan Record Store—but had no records to deliver to them. He may still have been slim with a full head of hair, but he was getting very old very fast. He finally had a record that people wanted to buy, but didn't have any copies to sell to them. In his notes he alludes to a nervous breakdown being a very real possibility. "My heart is actually breaking," he lamented.

A company in New Jersey promised to press the records, but they took more than two weeks to inform Ben that a key piece of equipment was in disrepair, and that the records wouldn't be pressed until the problem could be fixed. Ben wasn't eating. He found himself hiding away in corners to cry. He was frightened at his own behavior.

On August 14, a month since the orders first started coming in, he began to receive records and quickly sold more than a thousand. This gave him the impetus, and the cash, to cut a few more records, but this time he wanted as much control as possible over the entire process, so he quickly formulated plans to build an even more complete basement studio. He tried to get bank financing to help him purchase more equipment than he could afford on his own, but was turned down.

Meanwhile, "Take a Ship for Yourself" began selling well in Milwaukee, Chicago and other cities. He continued to bombard the market with advertising cards, each one more boastful and beseeching than the next. He also placed small promotional ads in industry trade papers which, in turn, were happy to run notices about the song's success. *The Coin Machine Journal* wrote in an April 1939 edition, "Benny Bell of the Radio Records Company has been doing quite a job with his record,

'The Boat Song.' Requests as to where this record could be purchased have been pouring in right along. Well, the answer is in this month's advertising columns of *The Coin Machine Journal*. This record is called a real surprise 'you-figure-it-out' novelty hit by Benny Bell and is played by Frank 'Miggs' Rand and his band. Some operators have purchased the record in tremendously large quantity and report that it is bringing in the nickels as speedily as any record ever did."

"Take a Ship for Yourself" was a bona fide hit:

> *Every time we take a trip*
> *You always get my goat*
> *I like trains and buses*
> *But you like a ferry boat*
> *Well, the next time we go traveling*
> *Ships are out and I declare*
> *You go your way, I'll go mine*
> *And I'll meet you over there.*
>
> *You take a ship for yourself*
> *I'll take a train by myself*
> *If you can't fly in planes*
> *Or ride in buses or in trains*
> *Then go take a ship for yourself.*

When the song seemed to reach the height of its popularity, Ben wrote and recorded a sequel called "I'm the Guy Who Took a Ship for Himself," but it paled in comparison to the original. The next record he came out with was called "The Automobile Song," a clever ditty that used car parts for double entendres throughout the composition:

Will you love me when my carburetor's busted?

Will you love me when I cannot shift my gears?

When my spark plug is as worn as Kelsey's doorknob?

When my clutch begins to slip will you shed tears?

Will you love me when my old exhaust gets rusty?

Will you love me when my pump is on the blink?

When my fender has a dent

And my piston rod is bent

Will you live me when my flivver is a wreck?

By June 1941, "The Automobile Song" was rivaling "The Boat Song" in popularity and sales. Following those were several other similarly cocky songs—"We Do it Just the Same," "She Got Her Tidbit" and "Noses" (which he also referred to as "Noses Run in My Family" and "Grandpa Had a Long One")—that enjoyed various levels of success because of their gleeful and ultimately harmless immodesty:

My grandpa had a long one

It nearly touched his chin

My uncle has a small one

With hardly any skin

My daddy has a broad one

Just like a rolling pin

But mine is big and round and fat

It looks more like a baseball bat

You never saw a nose like mine before.

While his financial future was still far from secure, at the present moment he was earning enough to pay off his debts, keep his wife and sons sufficiently clothed and well fed, buy more studio recording equipment, and even take out some stock.

With his basement studio nearly complete, he was as independent a music mogul as one could be. Other than actually pressing the discs in quantity and printing all the labels and sleeves, he took responsibility for writing the songs, performing and recording them, designing the artwork, advertising and promoting the final product, and delivering them to stores and jukebox operators. He was confident enough to go to the expense of having multi-sleeve hardcover albums made in which six Benny Bell 78 rpm records could be sold at once. Multi-sleeve albums had successfully been used for many years by all the major record companies for their biggest stars. Ben's six-sleeve album cover featured a picture of him in a sailor uniform, and two taglines, "For fun loving people, 16 years of age or older, who do not blush easily," and "Liven up your party, amaze your friends, a riot of fun, you'll laugh, you'll roar!"

By February 1942 business started to drop off, but he continued undaunted, seeking the next "Take a Ship for Yourself" or another "Automobile Song." But something happened the following month which started to rewrite his novelty story while it was still being written. A music dealer in Greenwich Village was arrested for selling spicy records, including some by Benny Bell. That worried Ben very much. (He gave the dealer some money to help fight the case, which was eventually dismissed.)

A few months later an acquaintance at the Clark Phonograph Recording Company phoned to warn Ben that federal investigators had visited corporate executives there to discuss the naughty records they were selling, and that frightened him some more.

Then, in September the Newark Police Department in New Jersey came into the picture. As the New York Times reported on Sunday, November 1, 1942, "A campaign against dealers in indecent phonograph recordings was ordered here today by Police Judge Ernest F. Masini after four owners of radio and music shops and another man had been arraigned before him on charges of possessing obscene records. The judge also ordered a warrant issued for the arrest of an undisclosed distributor alleged to have 10,000 objectionable records in stock."

Ben immediately chose to lay low on the novelty front until the spicy storm clouds lifted. His discography took a cautious turn after that, with tunes being added that were decidedly different in theme, such as "Number One on My Heart Parade," "Two, Four, Six Eight," "Take it Easy Polka," "Meet Me on the Corner" and "The Brooklyn Bounce." Once again, his achievements were being derailed right in front of his eyes, mostly because of actions beyond his control. He was in the wrong place at the wrong time, and he must have wondered why.

Within the next three years, with his finances steadily decreasing, he found himself back on the street as a pushcart peddler. But at the very least, being on the street this time gave him an idea that, one more time, helped him regain a foothold in the novelty world.

SHOW AND TELL

As a teenager, having a grandfather who sang a song about "strolling through the park, goosing statues in the dark" was a gift because of all those times when I didn't feel confident enough to rely on my own devices to get noticed. It was nice to be the grandson of someone who made dozens of naughty records, particularly since I was too shy to be naughty on my own. And I had plenty of album covers with Poppy Benny's picture on them to prove that I was telling the truth, even if no one actually knew any of the songs on the albums.

But the gift was always short-lived when the other kids discovered that my grandfather's songs were rarely if ever played on the radio, that his records couldn't be found in any of the suburban record stores where everyone shopped, or that he never appeared on "The Tonight Show," "The Mike Douglas Show," "The Merv Griffin Show" or any other popular TV programs of the day.

Then, in early 1975, novelty broadcaster Dr. Demento and renowned New York deejay Cousin Brucie resurrected the old Benny Bell tune, "Shaving Cream," and Poppy Benny's spotlight started to shine once again. I was 17-years-old, a senior in high school, and while I was no longer as shy as I had once been, "Shaving Cream," now being played regularly on one of the biggest and most important radio stations in the country, made things all that much better.

Cousin Brucie interviewed Poppy Benny on the air, and relatives and friends called to ask my parents, "When did all this happen?" Poppy Benny received offers from record companies. He was busier than ever. I even got to visit Cousin Brucie in his studio high atop Rockefeller Plaza in Manhattan. All I had to say was that Benny Bell sent me.

It was an exciting time.

All the same, the novelty wore off before long. He became a one-hit wonder to the Bubble Gum generation.

It got a little harder for my own children. When my daughters Celia and Kate brought in Benny Bell albums or sheet music to school for show-and-tell, it was a tough sell. "Shaving Cream" was no longer popular; it simply seemed like an oddity from another era (which it was)—and not a very wholesome oddity at that. There was a lot more "Who's Benny Bell?" in the mid 1990s than there was in the mid-1970s.

Bonnie and I didn't want to push the issue too much, so we didn't depend solely on Benny Bell for show-and-tell. After all, a kid who brought in a stuffed panda or a postcard from Uncle Bob's visit to China was always a lot safer than one who brought in a record with "Six Feet Under" on one side and "Home Again (Without Pants)" on the other.

In 2005 I tried a resurrection of my own on behalf of Benny Bell's all-but-forgotten legacy. I updated two of his songs, "Shaving Cream" and "Jack of all Trades," by writing new, saucier, more current lyrics, and hosting a party at my house where I recorded both songs with our guests as the live audience.

The party went over very well. Quite a number of guests were familiar with "Shaving Cream." In addition to debuting my updated songs, I also made Benny Bell the center of conversation, and everyone seemed interested—although it was tough trying to explain why he never appeared with Johnny Carson, why he lived in such a cramped apartment in Brooklyn, why *he always used the same self-drawn artwork on his albums, and why he al-ways recorded in his dingy, second-rate basement studio. I already knew that he was a stubborn and sometimes paranoid individual, but at the time of the party I had yet to come across all the documents and journal entries that showed why he may have become that way. I was familiar, of course, with just about all his recordings, but had not yet made a critical analysis of which ones tapped into his greatest gifts and deepest emotions as a musician—and why he chose to ignore those as the center of his marketing strategy.*

Would I be able to answer all their questions today? I'm not sure, because you have to have been in his skin to truly understand where he came from and what made him tick. And that's not easy to do—without or without pants.

ROYALTY

The eminent lyricist Mitchell Parish was inducted into the Songwriters Hall of Fame in 1972 for his body of work, which included "Moonlight Serenade," "Sophisticated Lady," "Stardust" and "Sweet Lorraine." Within the comprehensive online program that describes Parish's extensive discography, the name Benny Bell is listed as one of the four creators of a wartime waltz published in 1945, for which Parish had co-written the lyrics. The song was called "The Blond Sailor," and it had been recorded by the Andrews Sisters, who did well with it on the charts.

On one hand, that means that in a roundabout but nonetheless completely legitimate way, Benny Bell's name is forever logged in among all the professionals in the Songwriters Hall of Fame. But other than a $25 advance royalty check from Mills Music, there is nothing in any of Ben's notes, papers or ledgers detailing his participation in the project. Nor did he ever talk about it.

Parish was a Lithuanian Jew born six years before Ben. His wife's name was Molly. He died seven years before Ben, at the age of 92. Throughout his career as a lyricist, he was represented dozens of times in motion pictures, on Broadway and by contemporary singers during the Tin Pan Alley and Great American Songbook eras. Ben had mentioned being an acquaintance of his, but never elaborated. "The Blond Sailor," with lyrics by Parish, Benny Bell and Joseph Leib, and music by Jacob Pfeil, was a fairly typical story of a sailor tenderly saying goodbye to his stateside love as he prepares to ship off. It was a quintessential Andrews Sisters vehicle.

The song had originally been copyrighted in 1937, and again in 1945. Just how much of a contribution Ben made is unknown, though the lack of any supporting evidence suggests one of two possible scenarios: The first is that Ben ran into Parish on one of his frequent jaunts into Manhattan, and Parish, feeling particularly charitable to the hardworking and often hapless Ben, threw a co-lyricist credit his way as a friendly gesture, even if the input consisted of just a word or two. (Parish did have many collaborators over the course of his career.) Ben, in turn, may have left it at that without any further fanfare, wishing to avoid ever having to explain just how much of a contribution he made. The second scenario is that Ben did indeed play a major role in the construction of the song, but declined to include it in his personal discography simply because he disliked sharing credit with so many other people. He may not have wanted other similarly collaborative projects to come his way. He wanted to be a solo phenomenon.

Whatever the real story, it must have been frustrating for Ben to have his name on a major piece of work in conjunction with such a successful artist like Mitchell Parish and not be willing or able to talk about it. And that was far from the only such frustration at the time, musically speaking. There were several other instances in 1952 alone when artists of some note recorded Benny Bell songs with nothing much happening as a result. Leonard Joy, a prominent conductor who had worked with

Maurice Chevalier, Dinah Shore and others, recorded Ben's "The Girl from Chicago" but never released it. Jimmy Hillard, a successful producer at Mercury Records, recorded Ben's "Lulu is a Lulu" but never released it. Georgie's Tavern Band, which had a long string of novelty records that made the charts, recorded Ben's "One Dollar," but it didn't go far. (Ben also recorded it himself.) Georgie's Tavern Band specialized in the kind of music that Benny Bell wrote. Their song list included "The Daily Double," "Deep in the Cellar," "Beer Bottle Symphony," "I Can't Spell Schenectady" and "He Put a Bar in the Back of His Car." With a little diligence, a little luck and perhaps a little more willingness to let other artists interpret his work, Ben might have been able to contribute regularly to the repertoire of Georgie's Tavern Band. But "One Dollar" was the only Benny Bell tune they ever recorded.

FOR THE RECORD

I hesitated writing this chapter because it recalls the one and only time that Poppy Benny was disappointed in me, and the memory always makes me a little sad. But if this story is to be an unfiltered account of our 42-year relationship, then the filter must come off.

Actually, the incident was so fleeting that in the overall picture I suppose it could be regarded as virtually insignificant. Still, considering that it involved the record-making process, maybe it was somewhat revealing.

While I recall hearing just a few stories about some serious arguments he had had with people over the years, it's hard for me to declare with any conviction that Poppy Benny had much of a temper. At the very least, he kept anger, or even disappointment, completely out of the realm of the grandfather-grandchild bond.

Except one time.

I was a teenager. The two of us were in my father's workroom in the basement of my house, where by this time Poppy Benny had been keeping some records and a small arsenal of equipment, one piece of which was a massive machine—more than 100 pounds and bigger than a car tire—used to make master recording discs. He was checking one of the mechanisms on the machine, which was stored underneath my father's work table. There wasn't enough room to open the cover entirely and keep it open. So he asked me to hold it open while he tinkered with something mechanical inside. Then he took a few steps away to examine more closely, and in better light, a component which he had taken out of the machine. My arm was getting tired, so I relaxed it a bit, partially closing the cover of the machine in the process. What I didn't know was that the arm of the machine (similar to the needle arm on a record player) was not yet in its proper resting spot, and by closing the cover slightly I broke something off of the arm. Poppy Benny noticed right away and became quite agitated. He shook his head forlornly, sighed deeply, and it was clear on his face that he was very upset. Even though I hadn't been warned that the lid had to stay fully opened, I apologized—but he stayed focused on the unfortunate turn of events and didn't respond. He was not happy. Apparently the part I broke was one that either was irreplaceable, extremely rare or very expensive.

Poppy Benny's passion was songwriting, making records, and the equipment that married the two, and my teenage laziness, at that moment, at least, threatened the very existence of that marriage.

Of course, he was smart enough to know the senselessness of staying mad or harboring a grudge, so it wasn't long before he changed the subject and moved on. I never did find out what happened to the machine as a result of my tired arm. On one hand I was glad that Poppy Benny loved me enough to render it, ultimately, an insignificant memory (despite it showing up here); on the other hand, wondering just how much grief I inflicted is something that has bothered me to this day. The only thing he ever wanted to do was make records. Did I stop him from doing that for a while?

Business Ties

Ben Samberg was one of hundreds of thousands of entertainers who had to turn to other professions from time to time to support themselves and their families. There's no shame in that. In fact, it is often a badge of honor, for it speaks of humility, conviction and persistence all in the same breath.

Between the ages of 18 and 55, Ben worked as a salesman, shipping clerk, stock clerk, messenger, vendor and a dozen other vocations. He was employed at apparel outlets, newspaper distribution and publishing companies, law offices, banks, financial firms and many other businesses throughout New York City. Most of the jobs lasted only a few weeks, some only a few days. It is quite likely that his mind was always on things other than the job at hand.

Still, he was as interested in making a lot of money (as opposed to merely making ends meet) as anyone else and, given a choice, would most certainly have preferred making it in music instead of in apparel and newspaper distribution. And he did, in fact, have some grand schemes, eager plans and majestic ideas related to his musical and novelty activities. But he lacked the intellectual capital necessary to stand the true tests of commerce and finance and to give his plans a fighting chance. He was built of a different cloth. Or, if he did have what it took to navigate the world of finance, he either chose to ignore it or never realized he had it in the first place.

When Eli Oberstein made his comment about the record marketing potential of jukeboxes, he may simply have been suggesting that Ben try to write the kind of songs that would work well in that market and then seek out a company that might like to consider handling the rest (maybe even RCA, where Oberstein worked). But that's not how Ben took the suggestion. He wondered why the established record companies had to have a monopoly on all the coin-operated action. Why couldn't a one-man conglomerate take on the task, as well?

Ben thought he could.

So first he did a market test (which, ironically, *is* the way a seasoned business professional would begin the venture). He manufactured approximately 1500 of several of his own records (investing $150 to the effort), took them to 25 venues in various New York neighborhoods that operated jukeboxes, and earned about $1000 in jukebox and commercial sales. Believing there to be as many as 125,000 jukeboxes in operation across the country, he calculated selling as many as 200,000 records and earning at least $100,000 a year. But he knew he couldn't do it entirely alone, particularly since he had no significant savings. So he drew up a business prospectus and placed it as an ad in the New York Times. The prospectus put out the call for investors to help fund "a factory for the manufacture of these articles" (which is how he referred to the jukebox records). He sought $10,000 to open the 'factory,' and agreed to split the profits in half between himself and "two or more (not exceeding ten) investors." He wrote in the prospectus that he would incorporate the venture immediately and begin distributing product to the market in a matter of weeks. "I never really encountered any venture so prospective by proof of an actual test," he wrote.

Furthermore, he promised to share with all investors the sales slips, bank deposits and invoices from his trail run, as proof of its viability. "If you can have your lawyer present to examine these exhibits," he concluded, "it will be appreciated. Please respond only if you are sincerely interested and not merely for the sake of curiosity."

There are no records of any responses to the prospectus.

INSTANT LAUGHTER

In the early 1970s I attended a relative's bar mitzvah at a suburban temple not far from where I lived. Nothing in particular stands out in my memory of the affair—other than the fact that Poppy Benny was there. He was able to turn any event, no matter how droll, into a pleasant occasion.

At the conclusion of the service, the rabbi took the pulpit to discourse on a topic of his choosing. He spoke about our culture of immediacy; there was too much emphasis, he said, on doing things, having things, acquiring things and trying to accomplish things much too quickly. He wanted us all to slow down. He admonished us to avoid giving credence to books about major events that were published just weeks after the events took place, to savor the value of good, wholesome cooking rather than growing dependent upon instant dinners that could be popped into microwave ovens, to warn our youngsters against the dangers of instant gratification through drugs and casual sex.

Afterward, all the guests were ushered into the lobby, where the bar mitzvah boy's family, following tradition, sponsored a little repast of cakes, cookies and beverages prior to going to the reception hall. The rabbi was there. I stayed close to Poppy Benny, because that was always the smart thing to do.

With a plate in one hand and a cup in the other, he went over to the rabbi.

"I enjoyed your speech," he said.

The rabbi thanked him.

"And by the way, this is the best instant coffee I've ever had."

If there was any fire in the rabbi's eyes, it dissipated instantly as the irony—and the humor—sunk in. That was one of my grandfather's gifts. You just couldn't stay mad at him.

PEDDLING PINCUS

They were scrubby. They were cunning. They were poor. Some were wise, others foolish.

The pushcart peddlers Ben watched as a child filled him with curiosity and wonder, even a little admiration, perhaps because of how they got to see and be part of the lively landscape day after day, morning to night, on the Lower East Side of Manhattan. How he would love to have done that when he was growing up.

In the mid 1940s he got the chance to be one for real, for the second time in his life. He joined his brother-in-law Nat once again as a pushcart operator for a short while as a way to make some money after the hoopla around "Take a Ship for Yourself" and "The Automobile Song" had faded. But this time around he donned a costume and a fake beard because he did not wish to compromise the little bit of recognition he had won through those popular songs by being seen trying to scrape a few dollars together on the sidewalks of New York.

He must have looked like a throwback to the turn of the century, when immigrants with names like Moishe and Chaim roamed the streets looking to earn a few honest dollars. Fellow merchants began calling him Pincus the peddler. At the suggestion of a friend, he combined that

alliterative name with the kind of down-but-never-out characters he had
loved so much as a child, and composed a song called "Pincus the Peddler" in May 1945. He recorded it in December.

With a catchy, evocative melody (and a very flavorful arrangement), the song told the story of an immigrant who, with his beloved
father, runs away from home in Russia to start a new life in America.

> *I'm Pincus the Peddler*
> *A broken-hearted peddler*
> *The most unlucky peddler that was ever born.*
> *My mama in Slobodka*
> *Was drinking too much vodka*
> *And left me stranded on a Sunday morn.*

There's a sense of awe between the lines whenever Pincus, a new American (although not a legal American, having stowed away on a steamer),
sings of Mississippi and California, two states in his adopted homeland,
and then proudly announces: "I'm Pincus the Peddler, Brooklyn U.S.A."
But once Pincus grows up, he meets a woman who, while not a drunk
like his mother, is mean and heartless, and forces him to do things he
doesn't want to do, such as gambling at the races, where he loses all
their money. Things go downhill from there.

> *'Twas at a game of rummy*
> *She called me a dummy*
> *I punched her in the mouth because that makes me mad.*
> *She lifted her umbrella*
> *So I kicked her down the cellar*
> *And broke the nicest girdle that she ever had.*

She gets the last laugh, however, for it doesn't take much for the immigration officials to find an excuse to get rid of another illegal immigrant.

> *She went to Ellis Island*
> *To send me back to my land*
> *The things she told the people there were very bad.*
> *I never thought they'd do it*
> *And yet before I knew it*
> *They packed my trunk and sent me back to Petrograd.*

And at the end, he cheers for "good old Jamaica Bay," says "hooray for Rockaway," and sadly (yet somehow hopefully) concludes that he is still "Pincus, but no more in the U.S.A."

He told quite a story in just two-and-a-half minutes. Confident with early reactions to several live performances, he ordered more copies of "Pincus the Peddler" to be pressed than of any other record he had previously recorded and turned on the self-marketing machine at full power. Things moved fast—at least for him. In February 1946, disk jockey Martin Block played "Pincus the Peddler" on his enormously popular "Make Believe Ballroom" on WNEW-AM, one of the top stations in New York. In March, columnist Nick Kenny wrote about the song in *The New York Mirror*. Before long the record was being distributed to bars, clubs and saloons throughout New York City for insertion into thousands of jukeboxes, and record sales followed—by one estimate as many as 200,000.

Ben's "Pincus" project took up most of his time (which is inevitable when you act as your own agent, manager, publisher, producer and publicist) and he wrote only one other song over the next seven months

("Don't Throw Stones at Your Mother"). But it wasn't too long before he had the impetus to get back to composing and turned out almost 75 new songs in the next two-and-a-half years. The catalog of new songs, however, was a relatively scattered and unfocused affair, representing a half dozen different genres, themes and moods. Despite the success of "Pincus the Peddler," Ben didn't seem able to decide where he fit in, musically, so he decided to chase all the genres that he had tried in the past. His songs at the time ran the gamut from rags-to-rags ballads like "Barroom Serenade" and "Cockeye Matty," to bouncy novelties like "Valentine Polka" and "It's Bad (But it Could be Worse)," to Pincus sequels, such as "The Son of Pincus the Peddler" and "Pincus Went to the Mountains," to Jewish-themed and Yiddish language numbers, including "Kosher for Passover," "Calypso Mandelbaum," "Hetzalah Getzaleh Goo" and "Romania Romania."

While sticking to the evocative story-song format might have been a very good option, he decided not to. He may not have even given it much thought, occupied as he was with the running of his one-man musical enterprise (and buying some of his most expensive recording equipment to date). Approximately six months after "Pincus the Peddler" appeared on the scene, he wrote a double-entendre novelty song that soon made a fairly good jukebox showing of its own—not as big as "Pincus the Peddler," but enough to keep his hopes up. It was "Shaving Cream," but it wasn't his voice on the recording. That was a decision he made for two reasons: one, he believed his own hype too much and didn't want to be a target of money-grubbers who, on the basis of the success of "Take a Ship for Yourself," "The Automobile Song" and now "Pincus the Peddler," may have thought he was richer and more famous than Eddie Cantor; and two, he didn't want his real name or his most popular stage name associated with a song that stood a chance of being cited by the authorities as obscene. It had been only five years since 'objectionable recordings' had become fodder for official allegations and investigations.

So Ben hired a friend to provide the vocals, a performer named Percy Weinstein. Weinstein, however, was also worried about the repercussions his own career might suffer if "Shaving Cream" were deemed inappropriate. So he used a pseudonym, Paul Wynn, which was actually a name that Ben himself used on occasion, and that Ben also used to identify other performers from time to time.

Meanwhile, as his own publicist, Ben embellished with the best of them. Almost everything he wrote (or said in public) for promotional purposes on behalf of his songs was marked by boastful articulations that would have made Florenz Ziegfeld and P. T. Barnum proud. He referred to some of his songs as 'the funniest in the world' and others as 'the nuttiest in captivity.'

For all the boastfulness, Ben was not imagining the success he was having, at least on a local level. That was real. Between "Pincus the Peddler" and "Shaving Cream," he had earned more money, publicity and respect in 1946 and 1947 than in the all the previous years of his career. Ben and Molly bought an apartment building in April 1947 for $2200. Molly presented her beloved husband with a genuine diamond ring. Together they purchased a brand new, state-of-the-art Admiral TV set.

Too bad he never let any management professional give him the guidance that might have helped him actually make an appearance on it.

THE WIZARD OF SHEEPSHEAD BAY

*O*ne day in 1967 when my parents, sister and I drove to Brooklyn for a visit with Grandma Molly and Poppy Benny, we were eagerly ushered into the living room to see Poppy Benny's "new color TV." Black & white sets were still in use in more than half of all American television households. Color sets remained somewhat of a novelty and were still very expensive. So Poppy Benny's announcement did have a measure of excitement.

We walked into the living room and sat down on the couch in great anticipation. In front of us was the same old black & white television set that had been there for the last several years. Irene and I looked at each other. We were confused. But then Poppy Benny stood beside the set and flipped over onto the screen a soft, see-through acetate sheet with several rows of primary colors upon its surface.

"See? Greens for grass, yellows and reds for clothes, blues for skies..." Poppy Benny began to explain.

I had never been certain just how serious he was about that 'color TV' accessory. Irene insists he was sincere in his belief that his ancient black & white had effectively become a newfangled color set. I was never willing to make that leap. After all, he was technically savvy, what with all the work he had done with recording equipment over the years. I had even heard him talk from time to time on other scientific topics and, like my father, enjoyed having newfangled electronic gadgets and gizmos before everyone else. Benny Bell wasn't quite a closet renaissance man, but as a composer, arranger, singer, guitar player, recording engineer, comedian, writer, researcher and storyteller, he came as close to a renaissance man as a Pincus the Peddler can be.

As far as science was concerned, he had ideas but not the patience to look into them with the depth needed to make practical assessments. In 1976 he drew up and copyrighted a plan for transporting nuclear ash into outer space, where it could be safely released. He wanted to share it with public officials as a way of helping to solve a problem that, at the time, was a frequent news story. But in his schematic drawing the rocket engine was at the top of the ship, a design that would have instantly set the whole thing on fire during liftoff. I mentioned this to him when he showed me the schematic, but he was too tied to the general idea to be concerned with the technical details, and more or less dismissed my criticism.

Still, he was a resilient technician. Years later, when Grandma Molly was immobilized by severe arthritis and other age-related ailments, Poppy Benny fashioned a wheelchair out of an old supermarket shopping cart. He was convinced that his medical coverage would not allow for a real wheelchair unless certain conditions were met (and equally sure that they weren't being met), and he found it difficult to part with his meager savings to purchase a proper wheelchair outright. So he made his own out of the abandoned shopping cart.

It was very imaginative and very inexpensive. And also very dangerous.

But I Got a Lot of Fun

For Benny Bell, Brooklyn U.S.A. represented the top of the world in 1946 and 1947, and he stood proudly on its summit with the success of "Pincus the Peddler" and "Shaving Cream." Ben may not have been an Irving Berlin or a Johnny Mercer, but in those two momentous years of his career, his records were played regularly in jukeboxes at hundreds of saloons and soda shops and sung heartily by thousands of people at parties and on street corners. He was, for the moment, validated. He was a successful songwriter.

Which is why a letter he received in October 1948 must have felt like the summit had caved in without so much as a warning. He had very much wanted to join the American Society of Composers, Authors and Publishers (ASCAP), the venerable organization that protects the songs of its members and manages licensing agreements for airplay and other public performances. His idol, Irving Berlin, was a member, as were hundreds of other popular and successful songwriters, and he was ready to be a member, too, particularly since the successes of the previous two years clearly indicated to him that airplay and public performances were very real possibilities. But it wasn't so clear to ASCAP. After "Pincus the Peddler" and "Shaving Cream," his output of marketable and innovative compositions declined precipitously. The letter from ASCAP arrived at 450 Elton Street in the first week of October 1948:

> Dear Mr. Samberg:
>
> The Membership Committee regrets to inform you that it does not find the present activity of your catalogue to be sufficient to warrant your election to membership and that it is obliged to return your application.
>
> You will understand that this step is in no way a reflection upon your work. However, we find that at this time the works do lack revenue-producing possibilities. If at any time you produce additional works, or have reason to believe that your present works are being generally performed by our licensees, we shall be glad to have you re-submit your application...

It was signed by Membership Committee Chairman Ray Henderson, the songwriter who had composed "Button up Your Overcoat," "I'm Sitting on Top of the World" and "Bye, Bye, Blackbird," among many other hits.

The letter concluded with the hope that ASCAP may at a later date number him among their members. That never happened. (He later joined Broadway Music Incorporated—BMI—a competing organization that, at that time, had a lesser reputation in popular music.)

The interviews and radio and TV appearances that could have been lined up on the basis of the success of "Pincus the Peddler" were not lined up, because he didn't have any professionals to line them up for him. The money he earned could have been invested wisely, but it wasn't because he pumped too much back into his own enterprises and didn't have a financial counselor to give him advice and recommendations.

And then there were other issues, most of which had little to do with the imaginative world inside of him and everything to do with the real world outside. Though Ben was not one to let external affairs, domestic or otherwise, get in the way of composing and working on his commercial ventures, it is possible that some of the events of 1948 did indeed curb his creative vigor. It was a year in which his eldest son Jerry turned 18, got his driver's license and received his draft notice. It was the do-or-die year for Israeli independence, with which he was very concerned. It was the year the U.S. copyright office raised its rate from $1.00 to $4.00 per song, presenting him with new financial challenges. And it was also the year that Columbia Records introduced the 33⅓ rpm long-playing record format, an announcement that meant he would probably have to build an entirely new production studio, after spending hundreds of hours and thousands of dollars building the one he already had.

Jerry's draft notice required him to report for duty on Passover. Ben, who revered the Jewish holidays, went to a local congressman to see if a deferment, or at least a delay, could be effected, and a delay was granted. Jerry eventually enlisted later in the year and left for Fort Dix, New Jersey, on September third. Nine days later, Ben and Molly drove out to Fort Dix to visit him. Songs were important, but family was even more important.

Meanwhile, the 20 songs Ben wrote that year were cheerful at best (for he worked hard at always maintaining his sense of cheer, even when things seemed gloomy), though lackluster may have been a more accurate description. They included several feel-good hand-clappers like "Daily Double Waltz," "Let Bygones be Bygones," "One, Two, Three

Polka," and two that he would reissue at a later date, "Valentine Waltz" and "Yum Yum Yum."

The gimmick of "Valentine Polka" was the use of dozens of women's names in the song (which in later years he would modify to include the names of his granddaughters and great-granddaughters). Other than that there was really nothing unusual or intriguing about the song, and it certainly wasn't salacious by any means. "Yum, Yum, Yum" was a tribute to having no money, a theme he returned to often:

> *My mama and my papa used to tell me constantly*
> *If I work very hard the sun will always shine on me*
> *If working is the only way to get the sun to shine*
> *Then something tells me all I'll see is moonlight all the time.*
>
> *Yum, yum, yum*
> *Yum, yum, yum*
> *I ain't got no money but I got a lot of fun.*

Ben never had a lot of money. But we can certainly hope that he had a lot of fun. Given his professional profile, it's sometimes hard to believe.

OTTO'S GRANDPA

He had wit. He had moxie. He had character. He had energy. He had resilience.

And he had ego.

No one ever denied it—and if asked, he probably wouldn't deny it himself. Ego is a first cousin of resilience, though it is dressed up in much more immodest clothing. But it never seemed immodest on Poppy Benny. He was just too sweet and kooky to let it sully his reputation. Besides, ego is necessary in those cases where you really have to believe in yourself in order to stay the course. Certainly Molly always believed in him, but professionally speaking it just wasn't enough.

Perhaps I had some sort of innate sense of all this when I was growing up, which is why as an idiosyncrasy his ego never bothered me too much.

Still, it did bother me.

Before I turned my creative efforts to writing, I toyed with music, only because it was fun to pretend I was a little Benny Bell. I wrote a few lost-love ballads, with names like "The Girl that Ran Away" and "Someone to Talk To." One day, when my grandparents were visiting from Brooklyn, Gilbert O'Sullivan's 1972 hit "Alone Again, Naturally" was playing on the radio and Grandma Molly remarked that it sounded like a song that I might write. Poppy Benny, however, simply said that it was a good song and offered no comment on the comparison grandma had made. I was a little hurt. Two years later a popular record by country singer Charlie Rich came out called "The Most Beautiful Girl," and Grandma Molly said it reminded her very much my song, "The Girl that Ran Away," and that there was no reason my song couldn't be a hit one day. But Poppy Benny, sitting next to her, said nothing. I'd like to think he didn't want me to suffer the same iniquities he had suffered as a singer and songwriter. But more likely he didn't want to entertain grandma's notion—that I could have a hit song one day—as being even a remote possibility. Hit songs were reserved for him.

When I got a little older I wanted to write and act as much as he wanted to compose and sing. Ever since I was six or seven years old, nearly everything I witnessed, overheard, learned in school or simply wondered about I turned—in my head, at least—into plays or movies or novels, and most of the time I pictured myself in the leading role. When I was about 15 I started to write short stories. When I turned 16 I started to have articles published. When I was 17 I began auditioning for high school plays. I was beginning to pursue my creative aspirations as passionately and optimistically as he had always pursued his. I would have liked to have shared the experiences with him, but I was never able to in any real substantial way, and I guess I knew it all along. I knew that he was too narrowly focused to really give it much attention; in his perception, if something I did, creatively, strayed too far in scope, design or style from the things he did or the way he did them, it wouldn't have much of a chance for success. Also, I knew that he had too much invested in himself—past, present and future—to easily share the spotlight with anyone else in the family. Even me. I understood it, I accepted it, and yet it hurt.

When one of my first articles was published, my mother proudly showed it to Grandma Molly and Poppy Benny. Grandma Molly was sufficiently impressed, but Poppy Benny didn't even seem to read it carefully. Instead, he compared the style to his own, and commented on one aspect of my piece as one in which he felt he was a little stronger as a writer.

Two years later I was cast in a high school production of "The Diary of Anne Frank." It was my first major role. I played Otto Frank, Anne's father. My entire family was invited to the show. After the first performance, I rushed out of my costume and makeup to greet everyone up front. I saw Poppy Benny by the auditorium door introducing himself to people as Otto Frank's grandfather. Nothing about me. It was all about him.

I never once doubted his love, or his faith in my ambitions—not in any way, and not at any time. I just doubted he'd ever be able to show it.

THERE GOES MY COPYRIGHT

The second big Benny Bell musical mystery concerns chewing gum. In 1950 the songwriting team of composer Vic Mizzy and lyricist Mann Curtis copyrighted a song called "Choon' Gum," which singing star Teresa Brewer released in April of that year. Dean Martin and Ella Fitzgerald later came out with versions of their own. Mizzy would go on to write the television theme songs for "The Addams Family," "F-Troop," "Green Acres" and "Petticoat Junction," and Curtis co-wrote the lyrics to the popular standards "Let It Be Me," "I'm Gonna Live Till I Die" and "In a Sentimental Mood," among others.

Within a few years, "Choon' Gum" became a standard, an anthem of sorts, at countless camps, outings and other communal events coast to coast, and it still holds that distinction today:

Ben heard the Brewer recording of "Choon' Gum" on Martin Block's popular radio program when the song was first released, and he immediately wrote himself a note:

"There goes my copyright."

The following month Ben served notice on the company that published Brewer's "Choon' Gum," stating that it wasn't a Mizzy and Curtis original. However, there is no indication that he took any further action, legal or otherwise.

His own copyright history reveals a song registered in 1941 called "Choo Choo Chewing Gum," but the music and lyrics have nothing in common with the Mizzy and Curtis composition. "Choo Choo Chewing Gum" simply made play of the phrase "choo choo" by contrasting the locomotive sound from the name of the candy, and the music was closer in style to a pop ballad than a novelty ditty.

Why, then, was Ben so appalled when he heard Teresa Brewer singing "Choon' Gum" on the Martin Block show?

Because in January 1929 he had copyrighted a song called "I Bought Some Chewing Gum" that is *very* much like the one Mizzy and Curtis wrote 21 years later.

Ben had purchased a little writing tablet sometime between 1925 and 1928 that was called G. Martin's Writing Book, which contained several pages filled with blank musical staffs. (The opening page also had what was labeled "G. Martin's Rudiments of Notation and Harmony," a single, succinct lesson in music composition.) Twenty-six of Ben's earliest songs are musically transcribed into the book, including "Prepare for the Sunshine," "Beautiful Molly," "Coney Island Rose," "Rudolph Valentino," "I'm a Bootlegger's Son," as well as "The Bowery Bums," "The Bum's Rush" and "Sweet Violets." A song he titled "I Bought Some Chewing Gum" is also in the book, and in the upper right-hand corner Ben indicated that he composed it on January 12, 1929 and copyrighted it 18 days later. There are no lyrics—but the music is exactly the same as Mizzy and Curtis's "Choon' Gum."

It is indeed possible that it had been a public domain song from long ago that Ben felt free to modify. Or perhaps it was a variation on a classical piece of music from the previous century. Although copyrighting a modified public domain song is not in the same category as outright plagiarism, Ben may have wanted to avoid discussing his copyright in court, which could explain his decision not to pursue any legal action against Mizzy and Curtis.

Ben used to sing the song quite often. It was clearly one of his favorites, though we may forever wonder if he was singing an original song called "I Bought Some Chewing Gum," a Mizzy and Curtis composition called "Choon' Gum," or something created eons ago by someone else. But whatever he sang he sang with complete joy. So maybe it really doesn't matter.

GIVING THE WORLD A LITTLE GOOSING

In 1965 my parents took my sister and me to see "A Thousand Clowns," a movie written by Herb Gardner based on his Broadway play. In it, Jason Robards, Jr. plays Murray Burns, a television comedy writer who is fed up with the rat race and remains willingly, and willfully, unemployed for several months. The problem is that Murray's adoring 12-year-old nephew, Nick, lives with him, and after Nick writes an essay in school on "The Benefits of Unemployment Insurance," the child welfare bureau decides to investigate his living conditions and threatens to take the child away.

Nick finds Murray endlessly amusing, witty and wise about life and people and places. And Murray cares a lot for Nick, too. He wants him to understand why "it's worth all the trouble just to give the world a little goosing when you get a chance." He wants Nick to understand "the subtle, sneaky, important reasons he was born a human being, and not a chair."

Murray lives in a one-room apartment in Manhattan. It's merely a place to sleep after traversing the city streets in search of junk, like old clocks and decorative eagles. Whenever Murray needs a clean shirt he locates one still in its packing material in a drawer or on a shelf in the apartment. He plays the ukulele whenever the mood strikes, and Nick often accompanies him with one of his own. He asks Nick to read him to from the Help Wanted ads in the newspaper, and always finds a reason why the jobs are no good. "Nick, in a minute you're going to see a horrible thing," Murray says to his nephew early one morning, while standing on a city sidewalk looking through a pair of binoculars: "People going to work."

Did Herb Gardner know Poppy Benny?

For Murray, there are two choices in life: he could either be a loafer, or just another rat in the race. There's no in between for him. Yet, he really does know there are as many facets to one's personality as there are personalities, that people are complex and flexible and full of a million wonderful and wild possibilities. He even explains it to the social worker with whom he's falling in love, Sandra, who has some personality issues of her own. "Isn't it great to find out how many Sandras there are?" Murray asks her. "Like those little cars in the circus. This tiny red car comes out and putters around, suddenly its doors open and out come a thousand clowns, whooping and hollering and raising hell."

Murray was an enigma. But enigmas, like puzzles, can be clever, endlessly amusing, and even addictive.

I liked "A Thousand Clowns" very much. It's one of my favorite movies (and plays) of all time. I guess that was another reason my parents worried about me.

Like Murray's apartment, Ben's was a Museum of Stuff. Like Murray, Ben knew the city as if he owned every square inch of it. He and Grandma Molly took Irene and me on many outings, to city landmarks, to the movies, the planetarium, the zoo, just as Murray did with Nick and Sandra. Like Murray, Ben could turn any situation, even a grim one, into a joke. One story Irene and I love to tell is about the time Poppy Benny and Grandma Molly wanted to take us to see the Walt Disney movie, "101 Dalmatians," but the line was too long. We couldn't get in and were disappointed. So they took us to another movie instead, the Rogers and Hammerstein musical "Flower Drum Song," which Poppy Benny immediately began to call "101 Chinamen," to give it some sort of relationship to the movie we really wanted to see.

When he lived in his old Elton Street apartment, there were a few times he took me into the basement, where he had his recording studio, and it was a dark and mysterious maze of equipment not unlike the set of a horror movie. The skinny, cluttered stairway that led up to their apartment was a virtual storage facility for boxes and cartons and stacks of newspapers, books and magazines. For me, there was always excitement in the danger of climbing those stairs. I always had the distinct impression that my mother dreaded those Brooklyn visits not because of the people who would be there or the conversations we would have or the food we would eat, but because of the stairs we had to climb to get there.

We visited the Elton Street apartment, and later the one on East 16th Street, several times a year, and Grandma Molly and Poppy Benny visited our home in Westbury at least twice a month, always on Sunday. And even when there were no actual visits, there was still a Poppy Benny presence in our house each week because of "The Lawrence Welk Show," which he loved. The show, which aired on ABC throughout the 1960s, was a throwback to a type of entertainment that was quickly going out of vogue in that decade, yet it had a national spotlight every week, and I suspect my grandfather felt a vicarious justification in it—as if the possibility always existed for his own out-of-step styles to get a spotlight, as well. He never missed a Saturday night episode. He was particularly enamored of the piano player, Jo Ann Castle, who had a solo in every show. He wanted us to share in his delight, so he would dial our telephone number just as Jo Ann Castle was about to begin her performance, let the phone ring once to warn us, and then hang up.

So in a way, Poppy Benny was with us every Saturday night.

At the end of "A Thousand Clowns," Murray accepts an offer to return to his old job as head writer for the "Chuckles the Chipmunk" TV program. Perhaps he has finally accepted the notion that he can adapt while still making the most of his life, despite the job—that just because he lets out some of those thousand clowns, he doesn't have to give up who he really is inside.

Poppy Benny also gave the world a little goosing, just by living his life the way he wanted to. It made him happy. So maybe it's a good thing he never accepted other offers.

Then again, there really weren't many offers.

A Song is a Song

A nd then there was "Ship Ahoy, Sailor Boy."

"Ship Ahoy, Sailor Boy" was a war-time romance Ben wrote in 1950, and he managed to sell it to Mercury Records, which selected it as a single for Rose Marie, the singer-actress who later had her career-defining role as Sally Rogers on "The Dick Van Dyke Show." Ben was never actually introduced to Rose Marie, but she has been quoted as saying that she enjoyed recording the song and would have liked to have met the songwriter. Recorded for Mercury with Hal Hastings and his Orchestra, "Ship Ahoy, Sailor Boy" was a good-natured and well-produced record that may have fared much better a few years earlier when the country was still fully engaged in World War II:

> *One day while walking merrily*
> *A sailor said hello to me*
> *I said goodbye like a good girl should*
> *But he followed me like I knew he would.*
>
> *Ship ahoy, sailor boy*
> *On the briny sea*
> *Ship ahoy, sailor boy*
> *But come home safe to me.*

In February 1952 Ben heard Doris Day on the radio singing a song called "A Guy is a Guy," a new record that was written and copyrighted that year by Oscar Brand:

> *I walked down the street*
> *Like a good girl should*
> *He followed me down the street*
> *Like I knew he would.*
>
> *Because a guy is a guy*
> *Wherever he may be*
> *So listen and I'll tell you*
> *What this fella did to me.*

Though the melody differed, the tempo, mood and several phrases were remarkably similar to "Ship Ahoy, Sailor Boy." There is no record of a lawsuit, however, and that may be because Ben quickly discovered that Oscar Brand had written and recorded a similar song in 1949—a year *before* "Ship Ahoy, Sailor Boy"—called "A Gob is a Slob," on which the Doris Day number was closely modeled. It was said at the time that "A Gob is a Slob" used traditional lyrics from an old camp song:

> *Well, I walked down the street like a good girl should*
> *He followed me down the street like I knew he would*
> *Because a gob is a slob wherever he may be*
> *Listen and I'll tell you what this sailor did to me.*

Once again, Ben had borrowed some expressions from the public domain, as had Oscar Brand himself, but this time, in contrast to his experiences with "Sweet Violets" and "I Bought Some Chewing Gum," he was beaten to the punch by a year. When he renewed the copyright in 1979, he noted on the copyright form that he was the author of the music and lyrics with the exception "of the phrases 'like a good girl should' and 'as I knew he would,' which appear in an old traditional camp song."

Had he wanted to initiate a lawsuit in 1952 he would probably have been advised against it, primarily because intentional plagiarism is always difficult to prove in court. Perhaps, too, he didn't want anyone to point out that in the 1940s Irving Berlin wrote a song called "I Threw a Kiss in the Ocean," which was recorded by Peggy Lee and contained the lines, "From the ocean a kiss came back, 'twas my blue jacket answering me: ship ahoy, ship ahoy, ship ahoy, sailor boy, ship ahoy."

Berlin was as self-absorbed and suspicious as Ben (in some ways much more so), and ferociously protective of his own words and music. He once tried to sue *Mad* magazine for printing parody lyrics of his song "Cheek to Cheek." It's actually a bit surprising that Berlin didn't decide to take Ben to court for plagiarizing a key lyric. That wouldn't have been a particularly pleasant way for Ben to finally meet his idol face to face. In fact, it's probably a good thing that "Ship Ahoy, Sailor Boy" didn't sail very far on the charts.

Benny Bell and his "Portable Orchestra."

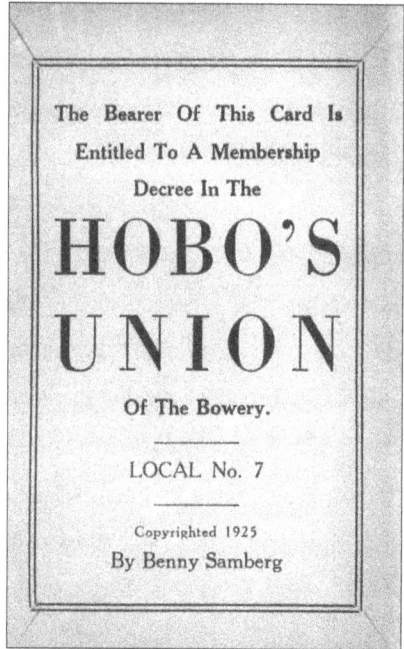

The Bearer Of This Card Is
Entitled To A Membership
Decree In The

HOBO'S UNION

Of The Bowery.

———

LOCAL No. 7

———

Copyrighted 1925
By Benny Samberg

Ben's first published literary gimmick: a self-help pamphlet for bums.

Hobo Jack Turner (right), a popular 'hillbilly' singer of the 1920s and '30s, recorded three of Ben's early 'bum' songs.

A little Benny Bell on Long Island? Author Joel Samberg.

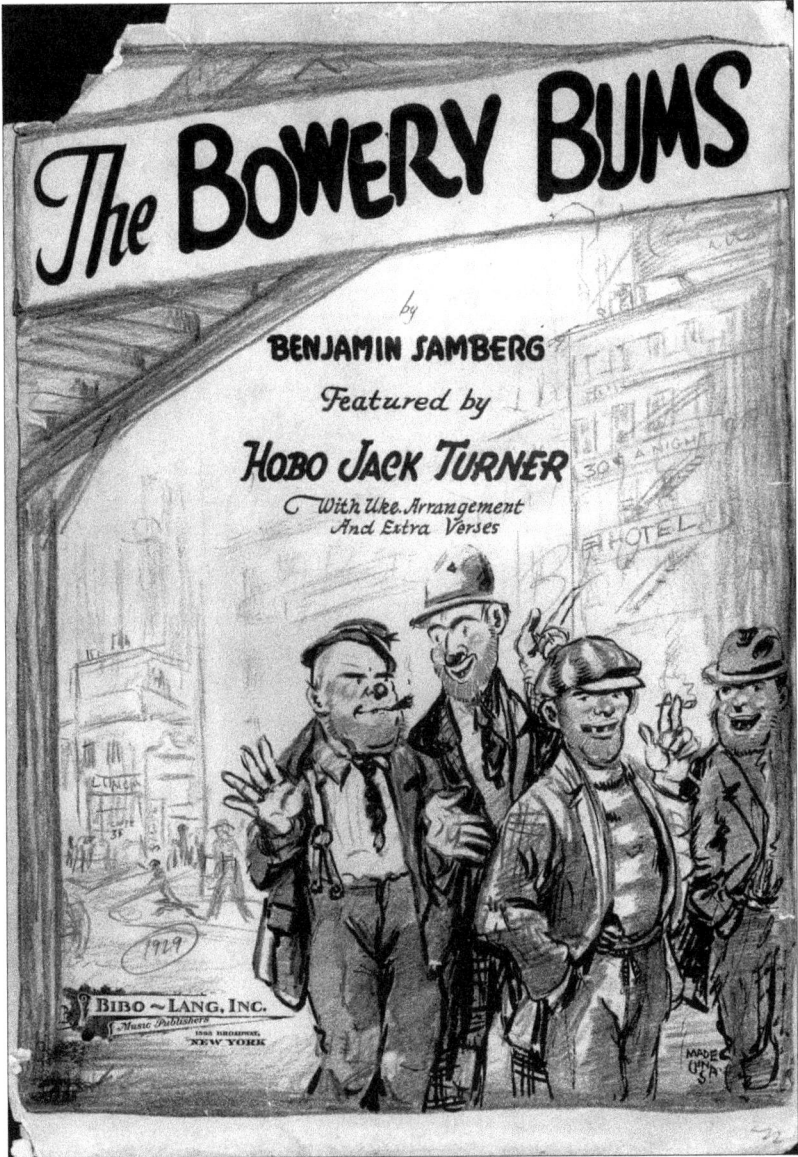

The sheet music for one of Ben's first professionally produced and recorded songs.

Ben, interviewed on WNBC-TV's "News 4 New York," made sure Molly was right beside him—and she always was.

Benjamin Samberg, soon to be more popularly known as Benny Bell.

Twelve years before becoming Sally Rogers on *The Dick Van Dyke Show*,
singer/actress Rose Marie recorded one of Ben's songs for Mercury Records.

BENNY BELL presents

The Best In Yiddish and English Comedy

— Have You Got ALL of These? —

Yiddish-Language

120 Benny Blesses A Bride
Misfortune

332 A Disgusted Millionaire
Elope With Me

246 Oy Could He Dahvin!
Russo-Polski Mazurka

390 Yiddish Radio Broadcast
Wedding Waltz

740 Ginger and Spice (Eye-yi)
Happiness Fraylech

— Special ENGLISH-JEWISH Version —
460 ROMANIA, ROMANIA
Oy D'Veiber

434 MOISHE PIPICK
In The Subway

516 Calypso Mandelbaum
Song Of Peace

638 Bar Mitzveh Speech
Celebration Fraylech

385 Helzaleh Getzaleh Goo
Gelt, Gelt, Gelt

415 Mozzle Tuff M'chitten
Hebrew School

English-Language

✓ 963 Dr. Yookle Kupvaytig
No Chiseling

✓ 591 Living and Laughing
Hungarian Chod'esh

★★ 523 PINCUS the PEDDLER
Why Buy A Cow?

★★ 230 The Son Of Pincus
First Hundred Years

★ 413 Pincus in the Mountains
A Disgusted Millionaire

✓ 952 McCarthy and McGinnis
Meet Me On The Corner

§ 457 Wedding Bells
Made To Order For Me

§ 810 Politics
There Ain't No Santa

★ 327 Pink pills for pale people
Hey Joe Two Beers

★★ COMICAL KIDDIE SONG
for Grown-ups (in Englis
2 ten-inch records in
folder-album.

Code-mark Explanation

Check ✓   A typical good BELL recording.
1 Star ★   Very, VERY good. You'll like it.
2 Stars ★★   Super-Duper-Special. DON'T miss it.
3 Stars ★★★   Sorry, we have nothing THAT good.
Section §   Could be better. Could be worse.
Asterisk ❖   Stinks, but if you want it, we have it.

An advertising flier for some of Ben's Yiddish-language comedy songs.

"Show me a man with two belly buttons and I'll show you a man with a navel reserve."

Benny with Uncle Floyd (at the piano) and Dr. Demento on the
syndicated "Comedy Tonight" TV show.

Uncle Floyd was one of Benny Bell's biggest fans, and frequently
shared that fact with many television audiences.

When he was a young man, Ben worked on his drawing skills with an enthusiasm almost equal to his music, as evidenced in this 1933 self-portrait.

COME ON DOWN

A Dramatico - Musical Composition

by BENNY BELL

Copyright MARCH 17ᵈ 1965
class D-pub #5761

Pub March 2ⁿᵈ 1965 Fee # 73799

Ben crafted more than two dozen vaudeville-style scripts that he hoped would be turned into TV shows—30 years after vaudeville ended.

Ben took the character of Pincus from his popular song and made him the star of this 1968 vaudeville-style musical-comedy effort.

Georgie's Tavern Band had a string of novelty hits, though their recording of
Ben's ode to poverty did not quite strike gold on the charts.

Ben's sons, Jerry and Charley.

Benjamin Samberg,
a.k.a. Benny Bell,
singer, songwriter,
nutty professor,
husband, father,
grandfather...

Mr. and Mrs. Ben Samberg, in the years leading up to their
new roles as grandma and grandpa.

Young Benjamin and his older sister Faye.

Ben and Molly, at the beginning of a love affair that lasted 67 years.

Ben in the costume he used for the cover of his multi-sleeve album set.

Sheet music for the song on which Ben shared co-lyricist credit
along with nationally acclaimed songwriter Mitchell Parish.

The teenaged Molly Ehrlich, shortly before becoming Mrs. Benjamin Samberg.

Ben could always be counted on to perform at family functions, such as this one in the 1960s.

Benjamin Zamberg and his little brother Sidney.

Four generations of Sambergs: Ben, his son Jerry,
grandson Joel and great-grandson Daniel.

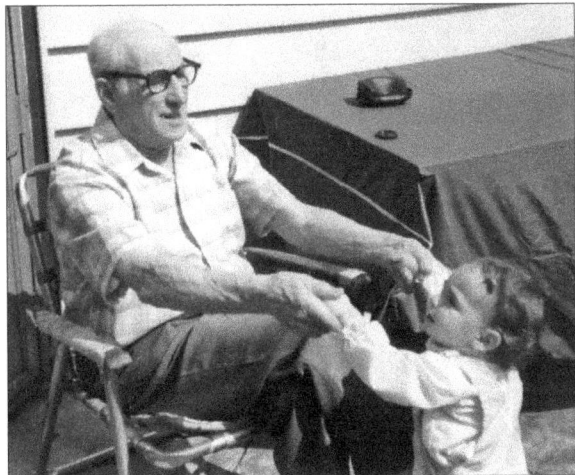

Ben with his great-
granddaughter
Celia. "See saw,
knock on the
door, who's there,
grandpa..."

Ben and Molly at the wedding of author Joel Samberg and his wife Bonnie.

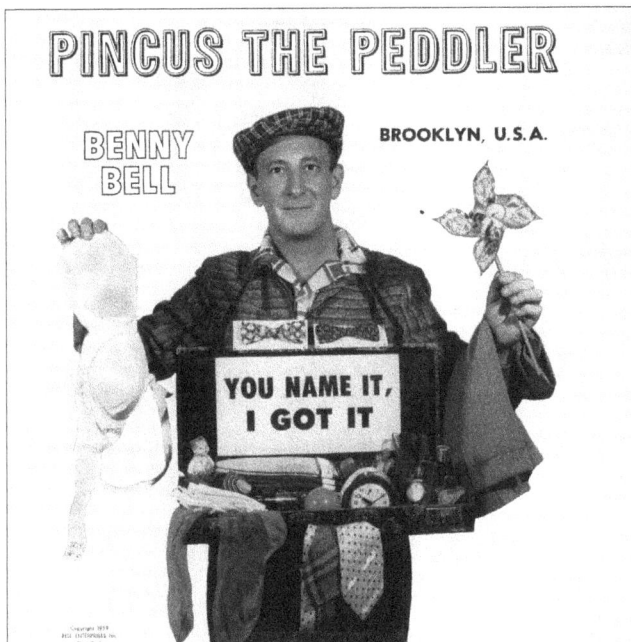

Pincus, the hapless musical peddler, resonated with
many fans throughout New York City.

At age 78, Ben threw himself a second bar mitzvah celebration. Many family
members and friends attended. Here he is with Molly and his two sons.

RIPOFF

To be Forewarned Is to be Forearmed So be Prepared

— o —

Butcher, Baker, Candy-maker,
Painter, Plumber, Disco-drummer,
Banker, Broker, Bellhop, Chief,
Anyone can be a Thief.

— o —

by Sam Berg

RIPOFF #33, page 27
The Smartest Hooker On Broadway

More than just another one of Ben's self-published novelty books, this one
described one of the deceptions in which he was actually entrapped.

The Vanguard album that followed closely on the heels of the "Shaving Cream" resurrection, thanks to Dr. Demento and Cousin Brucie.

Bell was just one of at least a half dozen names Ben used for his music publishing and record production companies.

From time to time, Ben managed to get his albums onto the racks
at some of the major music chain stores.

For the first time in decades, Ben had help marketing his own material, such as the sheet music for "Shaving Cream" after the Vanguard single and album were released.

A song with an interesting history, a wide reach, and several
recorded versions, including a few by Ben himself.

Author Joel Samberg's father and both his grandfathers (Ben on the left, David Mogel on the right) were featured on the cover of this earnest Jewish ceremonial album.

THE MOST AUTHENTIC
AND FACTUAL REPORT

On

WHAT MEN KNOW ABOUT WOMEN

Vestpocket Edition

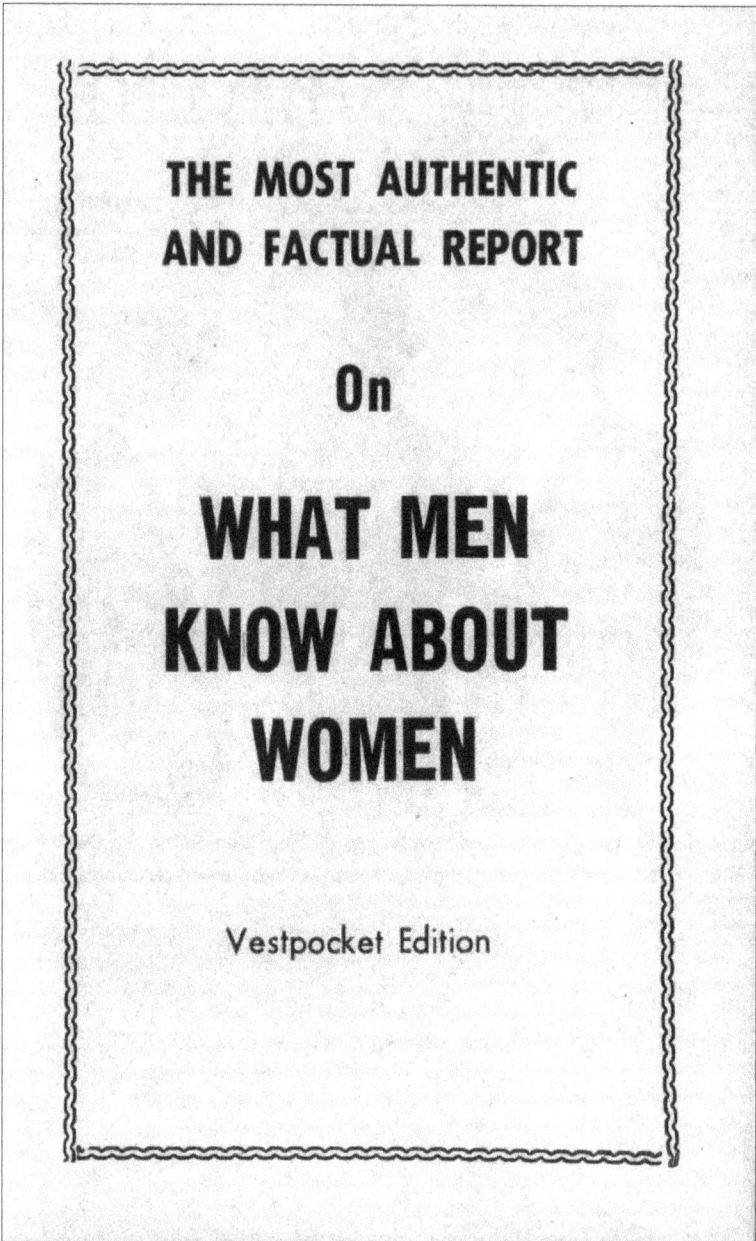

An early Ben Samberg novelty gimmick: all the pages in this little book were blank.

GEORGE PIANTADOSI,
GENERAL MANAGER

CABLE ADDRESS
"WORDMUSIC"

BRANCH OFFICES

CHICAGO
LOS ANGELES
PHILADELPHIA
DETROIT
BOSTON

WORDS AND MUSIC INC.
SUCCESSORS TO HARRY ENGEL INC.
MUSIC PUBLISHERS
1619 BROADWAY NEW YORK N.Y

TELEPHONE.

CIRCLE 7- {4094
4095
4096
4097
4098

BENJAMIN SAMBERG
450 Elton Street,
Brooklyn, New York
September 28th, 1936

WORDS & MUSIC, INC.
1619 Broadway,
NEW YORK CITY

Gentlemen:-

In consideration of the covenants and agreements hereinafter contained, I hereby sell, assign and transfer to you all my rights, title and interest in my musical selection entitled, I KNOW A CRAZY SONG (Chid-da Bid-da Bim Bum Boo!), under the following terms and conditions.

You are to print and publish regular copies of sheet music and sets of orchestrations and the name of BENNY SAMBER - - - to appear as the author of the words and music on the title page of each such copy. Publication of said sheet music and orchestrations are to commence within a period of sixty (60) days after the date of this assignment.

You are to pay me as hereinafter mentioned, the following royalty: - Three (3¢) cents per copy on all sheet music and orchestrations published and sold by you. Twenty-Five (25%) per cent of all royalties received by you for the mechanical reproduction of said musical selection and phonograph records, synchronizing, performing rights, electrical transcriptions, foreign rights and folio rights, as well as on all other miscellaneous rights and publications which inures to you from the exploitation of said musical selection. Payments of such royalties aforementioned should be made to me quarterly.

Yours truly,

Benjamin Samberg

Accepted by
WORD & MUSIC, INC.

In the presence of

Ben acted as his own agent, manager and (based on the wording of this 1936 letter) legal counsel on all aspects of his musical endeavors.

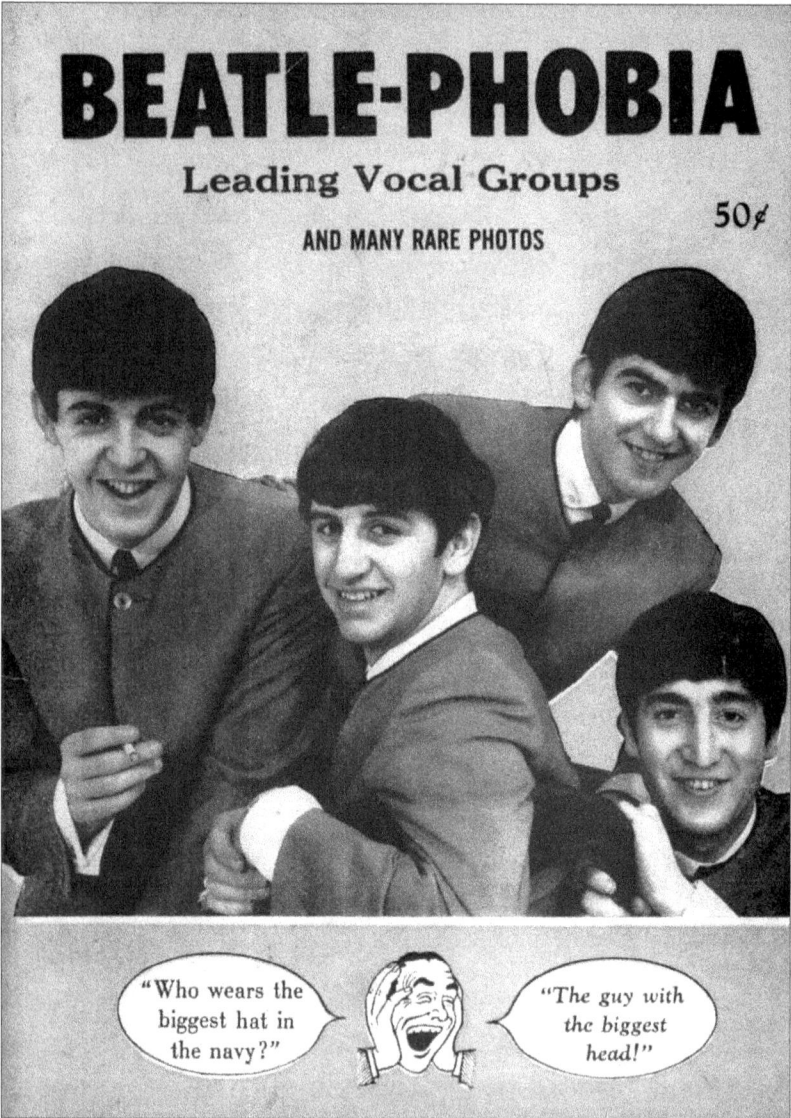

One of Ben's self-published books, put together during the height of Beatlemania.

AT REST

by BENNY BELL

HERE LIES MY BOSS
OH WHAT A GUY!
AT LAST HE'S RESTING
AND SO AM I

AT REST

Copyright 1956 Speciaity Sales,

Copyright 1956, Specialty Sales, Box 32, Brooklyn 8, N. Y.

From silly postcards to nutty certificates, Ben produced many curious items for the discount novelty trade. This is one of a series of wishful 'greeting' cards.

THE COP AND THE DAVENING

I was driving down Knapp Street and came to a stop sign. I didn't make a full stop. I slowed down and looked both ways, but I didn't make a full stop."

This was Poppy Benny telling me about something that had actually happened to him in Brooklyn not long before. "A cop pulled me over," he continued, "and told me he had to give me a ticket. So I started davening right there in the car. You know what davening is, right?"

I told him I knew what davening is— praying and chanting. I asked him if he was davening in Hebrew.

"Of course," he said. "I was davening and swaying back and forth a little bit right there in the car. So the cop gave me the ticket and I said thank you and drove away. When I got home I saw that the date on the ticket was wrong. The cop wrote in the date of the day before, not that day. So instead of paying the ticket, I went to traffic court. The cop had to be there, too. When the judge called me up he asked me why I wasn't just paying the ticket, why I was fighting it, so I told him that the date on the ticket was a day that I had stayed home. I didn't drive at all that day.

"The judge looked at the ticket. He asked the cop what date it was when he gave me the ticket. The cop told him the date. The judge said, 'That's not the date that's on the ticket,' and he asked the cop if he had an explanation.

"The cop said, 'I got confused.' The judge asked why he was confused, so the cop said, 'Well, he was rocking back and forth and praying in another language and it took me by surprise, and I guess I just got confused when I was writing out the ticket.'

"The judge turned to me and said, 'You were praying? In the car?' I nodded yes. "What were you praying for?' the judge asked.

"I was praying that he would write the wrong date on the ticket."

Poppy Benny was a born storyteller. He wasn't a one-liner like Henny Youngman or an instinctive ad-libber like Milton Berle, but was closer in type to Myron Cohen, who told stories in a warm, understated fashion. Cohen, born in Grodno, Poland, was a traveling salesman for many years before deciding to go into show business. He was almost fifty when he came to prominence in the 1950s, first on "The Kate Smith Hour" on television, and then on "The Ed Sullivan Show," where he subsequently made many appearances. He was also a Catskill regular, and two of his albums, "Everybody Gotta Be Someplace" and "It's Not a Question," were very popular.

Many of Cohen's stories were based on his experiences on the road as a salesman, although for quite a number of them he simply took the seed of truth and turned them into nearly complete fabrications. By contrast, all of my grandfather's stories were true, though so good was he at telling them that they seemed to be made-up routines.

It occurred to me only after I had reached adulthood that being a professional storyteller could have been a legitimate new road to success for my grandfather, had he thought of it, worked at it, stayed true to his core personality and welcomed a management professional or two to guide him along the way. But by the time I started to think about it, it was too late for him to effectively make the change, and I never did discuss it with him.

Not that he would have listened to me anyway.

To Unwind a Scatterbrain

Pincus—both the fictional peddler and the bittersweet ballad about him—was known by hundreds of thousands of people in and around New York in 1946. You would think that the composer and performer would want to stick to a winning formula.

Pincus was one of those Bowery characters Ben marveled at as a kid and had a fondness for recounting in words and music as an adult. There undoubtedly were more stories where "Pincus the Peddler" came from—dozens if not hundreds of stories, both real and imagined. More than just "Pincus" sequels, Ben could have developed story-songs about all the poor, tired, hungry masses he observed from his Lower East stomping grounds as a young adult.

With "Pincus the Peddler" his abilities as an arranger were also at a peak, and he could possibly have developed that skill even further. Ethnic-flavored tunes were his forte.

But that wasn't part of his plan.

Instead, he decided to chase whichever muse happened to inspire him in any particular month, even if not musically-oriented, rather than concentrating on a specific genre as a composer and performer. It is likely he thought that following a single path was a sure way of colliding with music industry personnel who would try to insert themselves into his career in ways he wanted no one inserted. He mistrusted almost everyone, was very impatient—but also very confident. If an idea popped into his head, he was certain it was a million-dollar idea that required immediate action, no matter how far removed from Pincus it was.

That is why for Ben Samberg the 1950s and '60s were marked by some of most unusual and eclectic series of projects and schemes of his entire career. They included concept albums, television skits, novelty books, marketing gimmicks, classified ads and more. Paraphrasing one of his own peddler skits, you name it, he did it.

In addition to all this activity, the era was marked by a full, sometimes edgy and never-dull family life. Between 1950 and 1954 his beloved Molly would be in and out of hospitals several times for a hysterectomy, pleurisy, opened internal stitches and various other ailments. His oldest son, Jerry, would be married by 1952, and his younger boy, Charley, the following year. Four grandchildren would arrive all within a six-year span between 1954 and 1960. And on top of all that activity, Ben was forced to initiate legal action on two separate occasions.

Life certainly was never dull for the comic peddler of Elton Street.

In October 1953 he sued the publishing giant Simon & Schuster, which at the time owned a record company subsidiary called Bell Records. Ben had registered the name Bell Records in December 1946 and produced many recordings on that label. It was a David and Goliath case in which Goliath could simply claim not to have known about the plaintiff's little company, which was not nationally known and had just one client.

Ben did win the lawsuit, however, and was awarded $4000. Simon & Schuster was enough of a goliath, however, to be able to make it a condition of the settlement that Ben had to relinquish his claim to the Bell Records name, and so the following year he registered it as Bell Enterprises instead.

Then, in the summer of 1960 he began noticing advertisements in the trade papers for Madison Records, a label that at that time had several popular songs on the charts by the Bell Notes ("Shortnin' Bread"), the Viscounts ("Night Train") and Danté and the Evergreens ("Time Machine"), among others. Ben had registered his own Madison Records in 1950, making it an uncannily similar situation to his previous one with Simon & Schuster and Bell Records. He immediately wrote a letter to the president of the other Madison Music, Larry Uttal, whose attorney was his father, Henry Utall, a partner in a law firm on Fifth Avenue in Manhattan.

"This is to inform you that your Madison Record label is interfering seriously with OUR Madison Record label," he wrote to Larry Uttal. "If you wish to discuss this situation before the start of legal action, you may call Applegate 7-3032 without delay and ask for the undersigned."

Attorney Henry Uttal's partner, Joseph Miller, asked to meet with Ben "for the purpose of concluding, if possible, our arrangements with respect to the above matter," but it took until March 1961 for the meeting to take place. The case was settled out of court. The terms of the agreement are unknown, though it *is* known that Larry Uttal folded his Madison label at about the same time as the settlement.

(In an interesting twist of fate, right after Uttal folded his Madison Records, he purchased the Bell Records that Simon & Schuster had previously owned.)

While all this was happening, Ben began writing a very odd series of short skits that he intended for television production, with such names as "The Crystal Gazer" (1952), "Life of the Party" (1954), "Nothing is Impossible" (1958), "Never a Dull Moment" (1960), "Benny Bell Rides Again" (1962) and "Slow Horses and Fast Women" (1963). In essence they were merely comic introductions to his songs (some of which were ballads), very vaudevillian in nature, and with very few structural conventions to match the needs and standards of most television productions in the 1950s and '60s. Actually, vaudeville still had a place on television in the early 1950s, before westerns took over in the latter part of the decade. "The Toast of the Town" (which later changed its name to "The Ed Sullivan Show") was joined by "Ted Mack's Amateur Hour," "The Colgate Comedy Hour," "Texaco Star Theatre" starring Milton Berle, "Your Show of Shows" with Sid Caesar and Imogene Coca, and other programs as seemingly endless sources of variety acts and skits. But Ben was not interested in learning how to properly organize his teleplays to even vaguely imitate the motifs of those shows. He was too tied to his own comic visions.

That's a shame. While there was little chance of Benny Bell ever having his own show, his vaudevillian style and even the diversity of many of his songs could have made the idea a viable concept for television variety in the 1950s and '60s. Although he lacked the effortless and instinctive skills of a Red Skelton, he invented similar kinds of characters (Pincus the Peddler among them) and often exhibited the same kind of wacky comedic sensibilities. In fact, unlike some comics of the era, Ben moved from the madcap to the sincere with the greatest of ease. One can almost imagine a skit in which he and his supporting players act out his 1956 song about certain death, "Six Feet Under," followed closely by another skit based on his 1958 song about absolute hope, "Nothing is Impossible."

"Six Feet Under," with its hand-clapping chorus and honky-tonk trombone, is perhaps the happiest song about death ever written:

> Ever since the world began
> Money's been a curse on man
> Work and slave and earn and spend
> Where does it get you in the end?
>
> Six feet under safe and sound
> Green grass growing all around
> The more you worry, I declare
> The sooner you'll be planted there.
>
> Rich man, poor man, beggar, bum
> Some have money, some have none
> But the score is always tied
> When they're resting side by side.
>
> Six feet under safe and sound
> Green grass growing all around
> The more you worry, I declare
> The sooner you'll be planted there.

By contrast, "Nothing is Impossible," which he wrote into his own TV variety script of the same name, could double as a Benny Bell anthem:

> Nothing is impossible
> Nothing is impossible
> Nothing is impossible
> If the Lord is on your side

Never say "It can't be done"
That's my advice to you
Hope and pray and try each day
To make your dreams come true

In the script, two songwriters, Sam and Jim, are working in an office. Jim is depressed; he's never written a hit song and is convinced he never will. Sam implores him to cheer up.

SAM: Nothing is impossible. As long as you are persistent, have faith and keep trying again and again, you will ultimately reach your goal.

JIM: Baloney! My grandfather followed those rules for a hundred years and died a total failure.

SAM: That's because he didn't follow the rules long enough.

JIM: Don't be funny. I tell you it's an impossible situation.

SAM: And I tell you that nothing is impossible. Didn't they say it's impossible when the Wright Brothers talked about their flying machine? When Edison announced his electric light bulb? When Fulton invented the fish market?

At that point, the two songwriters are inspired to compose a song, which they call "Nothing is Impossible." Then another character, Ben (to be played by Benny Bell), walks into the room. He's a vocalist who often works with Jim and Sam. He looks at the song the two have just written and then sings it to the audience.

The concept wasn't all that dissimilar from skits and songs in countless other variety programs on television at the time—but Ben was a little too selfish to share the spotlight with anyone else and likely would have balked at the requirement to have guest stars not of his choosing, a director to tell him what to do, and other writers to add to or modify his scripts. In short, "Nothing is Impossible" was a television show that was impossible to ever be produced.

He wrote his last two television skits in 1971, "Golden Age Follies," which he had hoped could be a motion picture (on the cover page he wrote: "26 million senior citizens are waiting for this delightful motion picture"), and "Pincus the Inventor," which was merely an excuse to show off a series of silly gadgets and gizmos that he 'invented,' such as a toy cow that dispenses milk "to fascinate food-resisting brats," and a merry-go-round hat "to unwind a scatterbrain."

In addition, through his own Specialty Sales Company he wrote and designed personalized greeting cards which he tried to market to five-and-ten-cent stores. He also created a gimmick called Lazy Correspondence, comprised of a series of oversized, preprinted multiple-choice postcards that travelers could purchase, fill out and send back home, without the need to come up with things to write about on their own:

I am staying at the _____ and having a ❑ wonderful ❑ miserable time. The place is ❑ nice ❑ lousy ❑ awful and the meals are ❑ good ❑ bad. There are ❑ many ❑ few girls, and most of them are ❑ beautiful ❑ passable ❑ ugly ❑ gruesome...

Ben placed classified ads in newspapers and magazines offering his services to write musical lead sheets for anyone who had an idea for a song but didn't know how to put it on paper (a side business he had attempted several times in the past). And he placed fake newspaper ads, as well, in an attempt to create a comic buzz about the joker who placed them:

NOTICE: To the man who stole my blue convertible. You may keep the car; I will not report it stolen if you will return the ten gallons of gasoline from the tank. No questions asked.

—BENNY BELL (Pincus the Peddler),
Box 30, Brooklyn, N.Y. 11229.

He also wrote several novelty books between 1955 and 1970, all of them self-published by the Specialty Sales Company. These included "Smile," "Beatle-Phobia," "Show Me" and several others. "Beatle-Phobia," a picture book about the Beatles that compared their popularity to that of other rock bands of the era, tried to capitalize on Beatlemania in the mid 1960s. "Show Me," a return his beloved vaudeville and Borscht Belt roots, was a compendium of show-me jokes: "Show me an Eskimo dwarf with a frozen finger and I'll show a frigid midget with a rigid digit." "Show me a man who wakes up smiling and I'll show you a married man who dreamt he was a bachelor."

In 1961 and '62 he was suddenly aggressive in seeking opportunities to appear on network television. First he auditioned for "The Tonight Show" when Jack Paar was the host (a young Dick Cavett was the assistant who actually auditioned him), then he auditioned for the "Merv Griffin Show," and once again for "The Tonight Show" after Johnny Carson had taken over as host. He never made it past the audition phase.

He did make it onto legendary broadcaster Joe Franklin's television talk-and-variety show a handful of times in the mid-1960s to sing some songs and demonstrate some of his nutty marketing gimmicks. In its 40-year run on several New York stations, "The Joe Franklin Show" welcomed more than 10,000 guests, from Barbra Streisand and Frank Sinatra to fringe oddities never to be heard from again.

And then there were the records. By the early 1950s he was producing long-playing albums—LPs—which had become popular in that decade. One of those he put out in this time period was a peculiar but not unworthy effort called "Be a Comedian," which presented complete comedy routines on side A, and the same routines on side B minus the punch lines. Only the straight man could be heard doing his bits, and then the listener was invited to deliver the punch lines (which would be followed by prerecorded audience laughter). The jokes were corny and the production values weak, but the concept was intriguing, and with a little help from industry pros it might have stirred up a little more interest than it did in the marketplace.

He also resurrected "Pincus the Peddler" for an album in which his old jukebox hit was surrounded by several other novelty songs sung by the Pincus character and members of his family. It was, like "Be a Comedian," a concept album of sorts, though years before anyone ever heard of a concept album.

In many ways, Ben was ahead of his time. But he was still too wrapped up in the past to notice.

THEY SAY IT'S WONDERFUL

The green eye scared me. It blinked in time to the music and followed me wherever I stood in the room. I told my parents about it, and they just smiled.

It looked like the eye of a suspicious cat, though it was really just a volume monitor on one of my father's amplifiers that he had installed in our basement when I was a kid, along with pre-amps, reel-to-reel tape recorders, turntables, tuners and several other pieces of stereophonic equipment. My father, Jerry, was a whiz at most things technical, recording and playback devices included. He was also quite a skilled carpenter who designed and built the handsome, wall-length mahogany console into which all the equipment was placed with great precision.

The green eye scared me—but the music it blinked to did not. While growing up I heard and enjoyed quite a lot of my father's favorite recordings, including those by Al Jolson, The Andrews Sisters, Bing Crosby, Dinah Shore, Perry Como, Artie Shaw and Benny Goodman, in addition to the soundtracks from "South Pacific," "The King and I" and dozens of others. He even had stereo demonstration records that made it seem like a racecar was speeding through the room from one end to the other. My basement was endlessly fascinating.

Often I would go through my father's record collection just to see what kind of interesting goodies I could uncover, and sometimes I would uncover something recorded by Jerry Samberg himself. That, too, was a thrill. They weren't finished albums or singles made for marketing; they were personal projects with hand- or typewritten labels. "They Say It's Wonderful," an Irving Berlin song from the musical "Annie Get Your Gun," was one that I listened to over and over, as well as "The Rich Maharajah of Magador" which was a novelty song that had previously been recorded by Vaughn Monroe. There were even several duets Jerry recorded with my mother, Reneé, one of which was "You'll Never Get Away," the musical personification of two young people in love—with pretty good voices to match.

With his rich baritone and mellow style, Jerry might have considered music as a profession. There was a Perry Como hiding somewhere inside him. A few of the pressings were even labeled "Jerry Bell and His Orchestra." He once told me that he had business cards made up with that name on it, along with a picture of a trumpet (which he had played as a young man). My father did indeed seem to have the showbiz bug when he was in his early twenties. And like his father, he also had the technical know-how to be a musical entrepreneur, had he so desired.

But that part of the equation is where the bug was quashed. My father grew up seeing what doing it on your own could mean. As a young boy and then a teenager, my father experienced what life was like in a Benny Bell-supported home. Then, as a homeowner with a basement, he had an almost daily reminder of what being a Benny Bell could mean, professionally speaking, because it was in our basement that my grandfather stored hundreds of unsold records that gathered dust in ripped and dirtied sleeves, and dozens of discarded test pressings. My father chose a career in air-conditioning and heating contracting, and he excelled at it and seems to have enjoyed the modest success he made of himself in the field.

Long before I had to choose anything in my life of great importance (other than which Matchbox cars to play with), I got to experience what it felt like to have a record of my own. I was only five years old when Poppy Benny recorded me singing a few songs, which he then transferred onto a vinyl disc. I sang "My Country 'Tis of Thee," and "Hickory Dickory Dock," and my sister played "In My Little Birch Canoe" on the piano. For years it was a badge of honor to be able to say that I had made a record, even if it was just for the family. I'm sure my parents didn't think it was such a badge of honor. They knew that while a blinking green electronic cat eye may be scary, being a professional musician can be downright terrifying.

Number 23 with a Bullet

Ben was watching television in the winter of 1966 when, at the end of a news program on WNBC, he heard anchor Edwin Newman wrap up a commentary by saying that "somebody should put up a prize for the first popular song about Brooklyn and Queens."

Within in a few hours Ben wrote "Brooklyn Bridge," a simple, affable tune about a fellow who blesses the beautiful bridge for bringing his beloved back to him.

> *Brooklyn Bridge*
> *I'm thankful as can be*
> *You found my girl for me*
> *The world is now sublime, and everything is fine*
> *Oh, Brooklyn Bridge*
> *My honey ran away*
> *But now she's back to stay*
> *Because of you.*
>
> *Her car broke down with a flat*
> *I came along*
> *Took care of that*

And then till dawn we stayed up
Kissed and made up.

Brooklyn Bridge
With all those stars above
You helped us fall in love
We're sweethearts again.

A few weeks later the recorded version was complete, with Ben as the singer and some of his ragtag yet competent musician cronies providing the accompaniment. He sent the record to Newman at WNBC, who was impressed enough to give it a big buildup and play it on the air.

Within days, dozens of music stores throughout New York City were clamoring for copies, urged on by customers who came in looking for it. The song "Winchester Cathedral," by the New Vaudeville Band, had been a number one hit on the contemporary music charts several weeks earlier, and many people commented that Benny Bell's "Brooklyn Bridge" was an appropriate response. As was his custom, Ben handled the entire production and distribution on his own, under the Madison Records label (for some reason he made "Brooklyn Bridge" the B side of the 45 rpm record), and it sold a modest number of copies—strictly locally. There was even a report of a Benny Bell fan club founded by a Brooklyn teenager who was smitten with the song and the songwriter who sang it.

Once again, Ben misidentified or ignored the promotional and musical options he could have chosen to build on the success of "Brooklyn Bridge." Songs about other New York City landmarks might have been a good idea. But he didn't write any. Instead, he continued to dabble with variety albums, various musical alterations on the Pincus theme, comedy skits for TV and novelty gimmicks. Another bona fide hit along the lines of "Take a Ship for Yourself," "The Automobile Song" and the original "Pincus the Peddler," all of which were now more than 20 years old, probably seemed like just a distant dream.

Oddly enough, it was a dream—a real dream—that *did* lead to his next hit.

In the spring of 1974, just over seven years after releasing "Brooklyn Bridge," Ben had a dream that he was standing next to a jukebox in a Brooklyn candy store singing "Shaving Cream." When he awoke he told Molly about the dream, and she insisted that it was a good omen.

"I think you should renew that copyright," she said to him.

Ben refused, believing there was no longer an audience for it, and claiming that it wouldn't be worth spending the money it would cost to renew—money that was sorely needed for the apartment. But Molly insisted, and so the "Shaving Cream" copyright was officially renewed in April 1974, which meant that if by some miracle the song were resurrected, Ben would still be its official owner and entitled to any and all royalties and whatever additional income might come about as a result.

At about the same time Ben had his dream, a Los Angeles-based novelty disk jockey named Barret Hansen, who went by the name Dr. Demento, came across a discarded copy of the original 1946 recording of "Shaving Cream," with the vocal by Percy Weinstein (listed as Paul Wynn). Demento bought the record and played it on his show. The program was syndicated in various markets nationwide, including New York, where it was carried by WNBC, a 50,000-watt all-music station. To help plug Dr. Demento's program, "Shaving Cream" was played in December 1974 on the popular "Cousin Brucie Show." That's when the madness began. WNBC Program Director John Lund recounted the sequence of events for an article in *Billboard* magazine. Here, in part, is what he wrote:

> *December 29, record becomes most requested song during WNBC "Total Request Week."*
>
> *December 31, "Total Request Week" ends at 5 p.m.. Tally of tens of thousands of requests tabulated shows that "Shaving Cream" was most-requested song.*
>
> *January 1, "Shaving Cream" is again played by Bruce Morrow.*
>
> *January 2, Bruce again plays "Shaving Cream."*
>
> *January 6, switchboard at WNBC is flooded with calls from listeners asking where to buy the record. New York's largest retail record chain, Sam Goody's, calls our music director asking where they could buy several thousand copies.*
>
> *January 8, during regular first-of-the-week calls to 40 record stores in metropolitan New York (to ascertain their top selling singles), 75% of store managers asked us where they could purchase "Shaving Cream." If stocked, we determined, the song would be top 30 in sales city-wide.*
>
> *January 9, "Shaving Cream" is in position #23 (with a bullet). Record is now being played on the station approximately once every five hours. Response is still overwhelming.*

On January 15, 1975, Ben was interviewed live on the air by Cousin

Brucie on WNBC. Brucie continually referred to him as Paul, as in Paul Wynn.

WNBC put Ben in touch with Herb Rosen, considered by many at the time to be the most important record promotion man in New York. The station also attempted to book several television appearances, including "The Tonight Show with Johnny Carson."

Ben signed a contract with Vanguard Records to release a single of "Shaving Cream" and to cut an album, also called "Shaving Cream," which would include nine additional Benny Bell songs, including "The Automobile Song," "Everybody Wants My Fanny," "Take a Ship for Yourself," "Jack of all Trades" and "A Goose For my Girl." Benny Bell was listed as the producer. In a way, it was 1946 all over again—except this time, somebody other than Ben was responsible for having the records pressed, the album covers designed, and the product promoted and shipped. Vanguard placed full-page ads for the single and the album in *Billboard*, *Cash Box* and *Record World*. The single sold extremely well (it reached #30 on the national *Billboard* chart, and one estimate indicated that a million copies were sold), and the album moved briskly. Several newspapers and magazines ran articles about the song and the songwriter. The *Bergen Record* in Northern New Jersey featured a piece entitled "Oldie ('46) Now a Goody" that recounted the amazing history of "a crazy oom-pah-pah novelty song." *Billboard* featured him, as well. "A clear example that perseverance can pay off," the reporter wrote, "as Benny Bell's 1946, x-rated 'Shaving Cream' single has resurfaced to become a leading novelty song of the day."

The song was also listed as a heavily requested chart-topper on WYSL in Buffalo, WIP in Philadelphia, WMEX in Boston, WIXY in

Cleveland, WLEE in Richmond, KWST in Los Angeles, KSFO in San Francisco and more than a dozen other major radio stations coast to coast.

Then, Percy Weinstein came back onto the scene.

Weinstein objected to the fact that he was receiving no credit, financially or otherwise, for the success of "Shaving Cream," 28 years after he had recorded it, and he seemed primed to initiative legal action. On March 30, 1975, Ben signed an affidavit that said,

> *"For twenty-eight years or so, these recordings were marketed by me with [Percy Weinstein's] full knowledge and consent and he never objected. In fact, he often reminded me and cautioned me to abide by our agreement not to reveal his identity as the vocalist and participant of these recordings...*

> *"On or about January 1*st*, 1975 the recording of 'Shaving Cream' became very popular, and in order to protect the vocalist from possible reprisal by his labor union, who might penalize him for such unauthorized activities, I continued to pose as the vocalist under my pseudonym of Paul Wynn. Mr. Weinstein, however, sensing an opportunity to gain fame and fortune from the benefit of this recording... has now begun to object to my taking his performance credit, despite our agreement...*

> *"Whereas Mr. Weinstein did not object to this course for approximately twenty-eight years, and whereas he insisted periodically that this proxy arrangement be maintained, he is therefore not justified to slanderize me now for impersonating him, as I was protecting him, at his own request..."*

There was apparently a small financial agreement and Percy Weinstein backed off.

But then there were more problems, which were all too reminiscent of some of his earlier experiences in the record business. Ben started getting sales reports from distributors (although unofficially) indicating how many copies Vanguard was selling of the "Shaving Cream" single, and he determined that it was a far greater number than Vanguard was admitting to—by his account three times as many. He was paid for 224,000 sales which, if the distributors were correct, was about 750,000 copies short. Ben claimed to have been underpaid by approximately $54,000. In addition, he composed and recorded 49 personalized "Shaving Cream" verses for disc jockeys at 17 radio stations to help with the song's promotion, for which Vanguard promised to pay approximately $2500. According to Ben, the company never came through with the money. There were also 25,000 copies of the single sold in Canada, for which he insisted he was never paid.

In all, Ben felt that he was owed at least $60,000. He sent a letter to Vanguard recommending the issue be resolved without having to go to court, "due to my advanced age and poor health." He added $15,000 to the total for "emotional stress from their unethical exploitation of my property."

(By this time, the Vanguard catalog had been purchased by the Welk Group, which meant that when legal papers were finally filed, Ben became a plaintiff in a lawsuit against a company founded by a man he adored, Lawrence Welk. Welk's son Lawrence Jr. was its current president.)

Meanwhile, what promotion guru Herb Rosen did for Ben is unclear, and there is no documentation of just how inflexible Ben may have been with requests concerning routines, itineraries and contractual arrangements, or with suggestions that might have given him more appeal in the often unpredictable and ruthless world of show business. The television appearances that were to supposed follow on the heels of the WNBC juggernaut never materialized. Ben had always hoped they would. On the back of a photocopy of an article about him that ran in *Songwriter* magazine, Ben wrote several new verses of "Shaving Cream" that he would have used on "The Tonight Show," had that become a reality:

They say Johnny Carson makes magic
At parties he's always a hit
He stuffs paper into his pockets
And pulls out a bag filled with...

Shaving cream, be nice and clean
Shave every day and you'll always look clean...

But he never got to sing it to Johnny.

Years passed. As he had all along, Ben continued to take a leading role in his own publicity with the kind of Tin Pan Alley bluster and gimmickry that sometimes make publicists more famous than those they publicize—but by now it was almost ten years since Dr. Demento and Cousin Bruce Morrow made "Shaving Cream" famous. The novelty had more or less worn off (except for die-hard Demento fans). One bulletin Ben sent in 1985 to disk jockeys and radio program directors said:

"That super comedy song, 'Shaving Cream,' has suddenly
appeared on national television featuring Benny Bell in person

*(the guy what wrote it) and it is off and running... Music deal-
ers will bless you if you join the disk jockey parade because,
even if youngsters tape it off the air they will also buy a copy
when they learn that the envelope of the single has many extra ultra-funny verses printed thereon which could make them
the star of any social gathering or beach party."*

The 'national television' appearance he was referring to was "Comedy
Tonight," a syndicated half-hour show on Sunday nights hosted by New
York TV personality Bill Boggs. Shown on approximately 120 stations
across the nation, the program held on for a while by featuring several notable comics and giving a spotlight to many newer ones trying to
climb their way up the ranks. Dr. Demento headlined the show, and as
part of his act he featured his own "Demented guests," which included
Uncle Floyd and Benny Bell. Demento introduced Ben as "The hit man
from Brooklyn." But "Comedy Tonight" was no "Tonight Show," and
after just 65 episodes it left the air for good.

"Shaving Cream," meanwhile, made its way onto a handful of records from other artists. A reggae band called Pop 'n' Mento recorded
a version of the song that ultimately appeared on several compilation
box sets; country singer Jim Nesbitt used it on one of his albums, as well
as on "The Best of Jim Nesbitt" in 1999; and Dr. Demento wrote several of his own verses for a few novelty compilation albums of his own.

The minor celebrity he held onto helped Ben deliver additional novelty songs to radio stations from time to time, including WNBC, even
without a major record label behind him anymore, or a publicist in front
trying to pave the way. For a short time, his song "Ikey and Mikey"
became the most requested song on a daily WNBC program hosted

by Michael Sarzynski. That song, too, was picked up by a few other recording artists (who were similarly on the outer fringes of showbiz), such as the Washboard Rhythm Kings. The song cleverly followed the word-substitution style of "Shaving Cream" and "Sweet Violets," and had a close similarity to a common camp and schoolyard verse, as did a few other Benny Bell tunes:

> *Ikey and Mikey were digging in a well*
> *Said Ikey to Mikey, 'I hope you go to*
> *Helen's birthday party, you will be quite a hit'*
> *Said Mikey to Ikey, 'I think you're full of*
> *Shish-ka-bob and pizza, and you drink a lot of tea*
> *And every hour on the hour you have to make a*
> *Peanut butter sandwich to feed your hungry heart*
> *But when you eat those Boston beans you always leave a*
> *Foreign letter in my mailbox, you're a crazy man*
> *Sometimes I get so angry I could kick you in the*
> *Candy store and hold your head beneath the water tap*
> *'Cause when you say you're sorry, that's just a load of*
> *crabgrass, my buddy, so if you're really wise*
> *You'll ask me no more questions*
> *And I'll tell you no more lies.'*

Ben dug up some other old tunes, as well, to try to peddle around, but with Vanguard gone and Madison back in, successful marketing was once more a hit-and-miss affair.

Mostly miss.

AS THOUSANDS KVETCH

Other than candy, it was nearly impossible to buy a good gift for Poppy Benny. What do you get someone who has nothing because he doesn't really want anything? Whatever he needed he bought on his own; his work was his hobby, but you can't just go to the store and buy a piece of recording equipment as a present. Who knows how to choose the correct unidirectional ribbon microphone with a rubber vibration-isolation unit for a musician's particular needs? Only Poppy Benny knew what was best for him.

He was too narrowly focused, too impatient, to really enjoy other activities. If you were to buy him a book, a game or a coffee mug with a picture on it, chances were he'd obsess for days over ways in which he could write one, design one or manufacture one that was better than the one he received as a gift.

As a creature of habit he even made it difficult for us to buy some of the daily necessities of life, like clothes. He wore only blue shirts. When I was a kid I don't remember a single birthday or Chanukah celebration where my mother didn't buy him a blue shirt. It became a joke, though he never seemed to mind. He knew himself as well as the rest of us knew him, and probably took pleasure in his own quirkiness. (I'd be willing to bet, however, that had we ransacked his apartment in those days we would have found several blue shirts still wrapped in plastic and pins, hidden in file cabinet drawers—just like in Murray's apartment in "A Thousand Clowns.")

When Poppy Benny's 86th birthday was approaching, Bonnie and I were determined not to buy him a blue shirt. We stumbled upon Laurence Bergreen's biography of Irving Berlin, "As Thousands Cheer," and our initial impression was that this was one book he would have patience for, one gift he could truly enjoy. We bought it for him. He seemed pleased, but in retrospect, I wonder if it were more a gift of torture than one of love.

Poppy Benny and his idol Irving Berlin (born Israel Baline) had many things in common. They were each raised on the Lower East Side. Their fathers were cantors, both of whom died while their sons were young. The boys had similar dispositions and enjoyed dealing in whimsy and fantasy. "He just dreams and sings to himself," one of Berlin's teachers is quoted as having said about young Izzy in grammar school.

Once they decided to become songwriters, both young men seemed to enjoy risqué parodies over conventional compositions. Berlin approached Harry Von Tilzer when he was 14 years old for a job as a song plugger, just as my grandfather had approached Von Tilzer when he was 17 to try to sell him some of his own tunes. Like my grandfather, Berlin used his skills for political involvement; Berlin wrote a campaign song for New York City Mayor Jimmy Walker and Poppy Benny wrote one for New York City Mayor Abraham Beame. And both had healthy egos.

But there were two major differences between them—differences that may have made my grandfather bitter, from time to time, wondering why his own success was so elusive. For one thing, my grandfather could read and write musical notation, and Irving Berlin could not. For another, Berlin all but ignored his Jewish heritage, while Poppy Benny embraced his, having always considered it an important measure of the worth of one's life. And yet, despite Berlin's inability to read and write sheet music and his lack of faith, it was he who was successful.

Ultimately, Poppy Benny was smart enough to know that it is an often inexplicable combination of talent, instinct, intellect, wisdom, technique, cunning, persistence and luck that's responsible for creating an Irving Berlin. For every one Irving Berlin there are thousands who aim for his level of success and esteem and never come within a hundred light years. My grandfather understood that. But he was also human, and it wouldn't be peculiar if he shook his head sullenly from time to time and asked himself, or God, "Why not me?"

And so, after Bonnie and I gave Poppy Benny "As Thousands Cheer," I began to question whether or not we had also just given him a new reason to ask, "Why not me?"

I hope not.

On the other hand, he may have decided not to read it at all.

BENNY AND THE SUNSHINE BAND

D espite his need to be imaginative and hang onto his vaudevillian ways at the same time, Ben had no misgivings imitating some of the modern entertainment trends in search of his next big gig, and he did it was as much glee as he brought to most of his projects. His problem in the 1970s was not resourcefulness but, oddly enough, true novelty—or lack thereof. Taking a cue from singing dogs, the Watergate affair and the disco craze wasn't necessarily a bad idea, but he seemed more compelled to jump on those hot bandwagons of the day before they cooled than to jump on them with a little more innovation in tow.

In the winter of 1971, Howard Smith, a deejay on WPLJ, a top FM station in New York City, played an obscure record that someone had found in a used record shop in Boston. The song was "Jingle Bells," and it was sung—or more appropriately, barked—by a dog. It had originally been recorded by Don Charles of Copenhagen in 1955, as one of several bits of songs on a single recording barked by a dog. The response was so good in New York that RCA immediately reengineered it and rushed a 45 rpm record into release by Christmas. In three weeks it sold almost a half million copies. Ben rushed, too—into his studio to record what he called "Fido's Wedding," by Benny Bell and Superhound. On the flip side was "Doggie Serenade."

The Superhound songs were not without some comic merit. In "Fido's Wedding," for instance, after the dog barks the wedding march, Ben, as the justice of the peace, says, "Fido and Fifi, with this ring I thee wed—and never bite her on the head. I now pronounce you mutt and mongrel." On "Doggie Serenade," Superhound barked the tune of "My Country 'Tis of Thee," with some additional comic asides by Benny Bell, mostly about Fido forgetting the words of the second verse.

"Fido's Wedding" was ready for the market just two or three weeks after "Jingle Bells" hit the charts. But as happens from time to time, the dog-barking novelty had already worn off, and Ben's contribution didn't really add anything new to it. Probably no one's would have.

Then, as President Richard M. Nixon was sinking deeper into scandal, Ben followed the lead of such entertainers as Mark Russell, David Frye, Mort Sahl, the comedy team of Burns & Schreiber, the sketch comedy group Second City and many others by coming out with a Watergate-inspired project. Russell and Frye were appearing in clubs all over the country, including extended stays in Washington, DC, devoting most of their routines to the scandal. One of Russell's famous lines was that the CIA now stood for Caught In the Act, and Frye was skilled at imitating Nixon, making him say the most humorously stupid things. Burns & Schreiber and Mort Sahl released albums called "The Watergate Comedy Hour" and "Sing a Song of Watergate, Apocryphal of Lies," respectively.

In January 1974, Ben wrote and recorded "Washington, Lincoln and Watergate," in which George Washington and Abraham Lincoln (played by Ben) discuss the Watergate affair. "Watergate was the name of a hotel that was bugged," Lincoln tells a confused Washington. "So," Washington comments, "why don't they get an exterminator?" "What about the cover-up? Was that wise?" Lincoln asks. Replies Washington, "Yes. Especially on a cold day, so you don't get pneumonia."

Then the vaudeville skit takes a curious turn at the end, when Lincoln suggests that because of Richard Nixon's efforts with regard to the Vietnam War, resulting in U.S. soldiers finally returning home, the beleaguered president should be given a pass for his Watergate-related indiscretions. That was a marked departure from the tone of Watergate humor coast to coast — not the kind of innovation people were looking for.

And then there was disco.

In 1974, the song "Rock the Boat," by the Hues Corporation, signaled what is commonly thought to be the beginning of the disco era. With roots in funk and soul, the musical genre featured mostly upbeat or love-obsessed lyrics supported by a heavy, syncopated bass line. Donna Summer, The Bee Gees, Barry White and KC and the Sunshine Band were among the many artists that brought disco to top-40 radio in the second half of the 1970s.

Benny Bell followed the leaders by making a few disco records of his own as the decade drew to a close, "Sweet Violets in Discoland" and "Disco Dancer" among them. Once again, he chased the trend without really studying it first. His singles did have a heavy bass line, but that was really their only connection to disco. "Sweet Violets in Discoland" resembled a samba, and "Disco Dancer" sounded more like a combination of bee bop and swing. In fact, the lyrics of "Disco Dancer" implore the listeners to get up "and swing again with me," even though the

Hustle is as far removed from swing as the twist is from a waltz.

Benny Bell was far too impatient when jumping onto bandwagons. But one thing can never be denied: he hustled.

A Thumb and a Bum

Benny Bell loved his four grandchildren and six great-grandchildren very much and, when he wasn't in his own special internal world writing songs or deciding how to get another gig, would spend plenty of time tying the joyful binds that make the grandfather-grandchild connection so special.

When my sister Irene and I were young, during visits to Brooklyn he would take us to a local playground, give us guided tours of some of the scary nooks and crannies in his apartment building, and push us on a little swing he had attached to one of his doorways. At our house, where there was a little more space, he would let us sit on his back or ride on his shoulders as he went from room to room, pretending to be a happy-go-lucky horse. He was too old to do that by the time the great-grandchildren came around, but his leg was always ready to give the little ones a see-saw ride while he sat in a chair, and he shared dozens of silly chants and did plenty of simple magic tricks, like making believe he could remove his thumb or pulling his ears to control the movement of his eyes and his tongue.

Being good at double-entendre meant that he never had to use a dirty word to be mischievous, and in all the years I knew him, Poppy Benny never uttered anything off-color, despite the fact that I was well aware of the sauciness of much of his material. In fact, the moral compass he brought to his role as grandfather was sometimes so sanitary that it bordered on the absurd.

One story that stands out is the silly little verse he used to chant about a person who was asked for his money, but the person's money was in his pocket, and his pocket was in his pants, and his pants were left at home. The last line of the verse is "You left them home? Get out of here, you drunken bum." But Poppy Benny never wanted to say 'drunken bum' in front of the kids; for some reason he thought it was an improper and sordid phrase. So instead, he substituted it with, "You left them home? Get out of here, da-dum-de-dum-de-dum"

So here we have Benny Bell, a novelty entertainer who wrote lyrics about nearly every body part and their various functions, yet would never say 'drunken bum' in front of children. What he never knew as I was growing up was that I was a hell of a lot more frightened of his missing thumb than I was of a drunken bum.

Successful Failures

As exciting as the "Shaving Cream" resurrection was for Ben in the mid 1970s, the experience had been sullied by more of the same record industry malfeasance he had suffered earlier in his career. It's no surprise, then, that one of his biggest projects toward the end of the resurrection was a self-published book called "Ripoff," which was a comprehensive anthology of incidents and events nationwide in which people were conned, swindled, cheated or duped, along with examples of hypocrisy and ignorance from all walks of life.

"This book is not a novel or a fictional tome for relaxed reading," he wrote in the introduction to "Ripoff," which he penned under the name Sam Berg. "It is a blinker with warning signals on the crossroads of thievery where deceitful billboards mislead unwary victims who really know better but are too busy or too anxious or too trusting to exercise more diligence when cruising on the Ripoff Highway."

Ben was an avid reader of newspapers and magazines. He cut out and saved thousands of articles over the years, and jotted down hundreds of stories and anecdotes that he was told or overheard as he went about his personal and professional life. "Ripoff" came out of those practices and, with some professional editorial direction, probably could have found a legitimate publisher. He seems to have enjoyed the research, the investigation, and the thrill of putting it all together.

No doubt he would have enjoyed selling it, too.

"Ripoff" was crammed with interesting stories. Like the one about the $20 mail-order device that could see through walls, which turned out to be a small hand drill worth $2.50 and a 6-inch length of a thin hollow tube to stick through the hole. Or the one about the attractive, sweet and accommodating young hooker who became a plaintiff in three paternity cases in three different counties, charging each client with fathering her unborn child. The men were married, wealthy and terrified, and the hooker was offered three large out-of-court cash settlements, although she wasn't really pregnant.

The book also featured reviews of other frivolous lawsuits, registers of idiotic laws and regulations, and lists of governmental waste, such as a $1 million grant to study whether intoxicated fish are more aggressive than sober fish; a $3 million disbursement to the U.S. Postal Service to create an advertising campaign that urged Americans to write more letters, and a $775,000 follow-up campaign to determine if the first campaign worked.

But one of the most revealing entries, toward the end of the book, is about a man he referred to as an acquaintance, who produced an album called "Showtime." This acquaintance wanted to test the album's potential with a small classified ad in the newspaper. After the ad ran, a company contacted the acquaintance to inform him of their monthly sales promotion catalog, which was to be sent to 1500 mail-order distributors. For $50, the acquaintance could have his album prominently featured in the catalog. Even if only a fraction of the 1500 distributors eventually decided to market the album in their own catalogs, it would instantly be promoted to several hundred thousand prospective buyers. But after the acquaintance remitted his $50 and approved the catalog page, there was not a single sale of "Showtime." A newspaper article soon exposed the sales promotion company as a fraud. Only 12 catalogs had been printed and distributed.

The story Ben told in "Ripoff" was true, but he really had no such acquaintance. "Showtime" was a Benny Bell album.

There were several other journalistic ventures Ben undertook before and after the "Shaving Cream" resurrection, enough, in fact, to suggest that Ben's literary ambitions were quite significant, although he had virtually no clue how to engage them properly. Writing was, in effect, another possible career that he relegated to quick-gimmick status. Among the yellowed clippings he had been collecting for decades were many about spiritual leaders who suffered unpleasant fates and houses of worship that met untimely catastrophes. He had long been planning either a book or a lengthy essay that would use these episodes to discuss a theory he posited from time to time: God was angry at mankind, or at least at religious leaders, for many reasons, one being the tarnish that man brought to the world's religions. The dates of the clippings ranged between the 1940s and the 1960s, but if he began a draft of the book, he never made mention of it in the files he passed along.

He also began work on a project he called "Successful Failures" which followed the fortunes of several businessmen and financiers whose ends were anything but fortunate. This, too, was either a book-to-be or a future magazine feature article.

In 1923 Ben read an account of a meeting in Chicago at the Edgewater Beach Hotel attended by what he called "the most dynamic gathering of world-famed capitalists ever assembled." Something prompted him, much later, to track their careers in the intervening years. As he soon discovered, Howard Hopson, head of the multi-billion-dollar Associated Gas & Electric Company, was found guilty of mail fraud in 1940 and was ultimately confined to a mental institution; Sam Insull, top stockholder of Northern & Indiana Gas & Electric and a vice president of General Motors, declared bankruptcy in 1932 and soon died penniless; Jesse Livermore, a Wall Street tycoon who wrote a book on making money in the stock market, committed suicide in 1940; Leon Fraser, director of the Bank for International Settlements in the 1930s, also took his own life.

Ben even went so far, in 1973, to contact the Edgewater Beach Hotel, site of the original meeting of financial minds, in an attempt to gather information to more accurately recreate the 1923 gathering. (The hotel had been torn down in the late 1960s, and Ben was unable to extract any additional information.) Ultimately, he dropped this literary project entirely.

He wrote a slim volume in 1977 called "Jews for Moses," which was a response to the Jews for Jesus movement that had begun only a few years before. (Jews for Jesus took out its first full-page ad in the New York Times in June 1976, which may have stirred Ben's passion.)

He also wrote several short articles and essays throughout the 1980s, though there is no evidence that any of them were published. These included "Medical Mystery" and "Houdini and Me."

"Medical Mystery" concerned his claim (through a tip from a friend) that a medicinal supplement sold in drug stores for $9.75 was basically just water and salt. But the article really didn't come off as an investigative or consumer advocacy piece because of Ben's penchant for adding humor to almost all the projects he undertook. The medicinal supplement sold in the drug store had an expiration date printed on it, and Ben commented at the end of the article that the *real* mystery was which expired first, the water or the salt.

"Houdini and Me" recounted his inauspicious meeting with the great magician in 1919, when Ben was 13. As he tells it, on an autograph line after a show, he badgered Houdini not for an autograph, but for a lesson in how to disappear. Houdini was annoyed at Ben's persistence and told him to scram—to run around the corner, thereby successfully disappearing. Furthermore, Houdini said to him, if he didn't scram, he'd kick him in the pants. In the essay, Ben's parting words were his wish that he had badgered the magician a little more. "Those pants," he wrote, "would be worth a fortune today."

UPLIFTING

It may not have been just Poppy Benny's stubborn paranoia that my mother and father hoped would pass me by. Maybe it was also his preoccupation with sex.

It's not that he was preoccupied with it to an abnormal degree; his could just be a little more public than normal, and therefore a little more problematic for my parents. After all, what were the neighbors to think if little Joel went around singing "We Do It Just the Same," "She Got Her Tid-Bit," "Two Times Tonight," "She's Still Got It" and several other similarly scandalous songs?

> She's still got it
> She's still got it
> I don't know what she's saving it for
> I still want it
> She won't give it
> I tell the world it's making me sore.

> The way that gal is treating me is really just a crime
> I come each night but she postpones it for another time
> She's still got it
> She's still got it
> I hope she'll let me have it today.

Ultimately, we find out in the song that what 'she's still got' is merely a library book, but prior to the punch line the perception tells a different story—which, of course, is precisely what Benny Bell intended.

Beyond the songs there were several other sexually-oriented marketing concepts through the years. There were at least three album covers from the late 1950s and early '60s that featured immodestly dressed (or undressed) women. On one, a bare-chested blonde had her breasts hidden by a small washcloth that you could easily lift to take a peak. But instead of an actual phonograph record inside, there was a round piece of cardboard upon which was written, "They don't make records the way they used to. I can't get a damn sound out of this one. Anyway, the cover is amusing, so have a laugh on me." Another album cover—this time with a real record inside, "If You Can't Come, Call Up"—showed a redhead in a lacy corset and a tiny mesh brassiere top capped with hearts, which left little to the imagination. Then there was the artwork he prepared for the 1957 album "Cocktail Party Songs" (although actual copies of the album cover have been extremely rare since its inception) in which a drawing of the naked backside of a woman is shown just slightly out of reach of a four-legged grizzly, and the caption reads, "A country girl with a bear behind."

There is also a drawing of a curvy woman in a bathing suit on the back cover of his 1969 book, "Show Me," which highlights each part of her body in terms of the accessories needed to keep her looking good, and in good working order, such as liniment and a girdle.

While I don't believe my parents made any concerted effort to hide my grandfather's more adult-oriented output from me when I was young, neither do I remember seeing or hearing much of it until I was older. So either they were very good at suppressing it, or it just went over my head.

On the other hand, I do recall that when I was 12 I began wondering what uplifts were. So I guess that's when I saw my first copy of "Show Me."

AIR DEMENTIA

It wasn't a wedding, or a bar mitzvah, or a wish to visit old friends, or even a chance to see Hollywood or Disneyland, but an invitation to perform in front of a live audience that finally prompted Ben to leave New York—at least for a little while. His appearance at The Comedy Club in Reseda, California, was really the first time Ben left his home state for something other than family matters.

Entertaining was in his blood, though other than amateur contests when he was young, several spur-of-the-moment Catskill recitals from the thirties through the sixties, and countless parties and family functions over the years, live performances (especially paid performances) were few and far between. A handful from the early days were nonetheless quite noteworthy, such as a 1942 gig at the Fraternal Clubhouse in Manhattan and a 1946 children's show for hundreds of Boy Scouts in Laurel Hills, Pennsylvania.

The Fraternal Clubhouse, on West 48th Street in midtown, featured swing and jazz bands with such notable headliners as saxophonist Dexter Gordon and clarinetist Tony Scott. It was also a popular venue for lectures and organizational meetings, some of them communist-affiliated, such as the International Workers Order.

At the Boy Scout event, Ben shared the bill with the Bunin Puppets, which was a very popular act at the time. Hope and Morey Bunin's puppets appeared on many TV shows, as well as in the 1946 motion picture "The Ziegfeld Follies" with William Powell, Judy Garland, Fred Astaire, Fanny Brice and Gene Kelly. One of the Bunin puppets, Foodini, would even have his own syndicated show by the end of the decade.

But it took another 36 years for Ben to reach a higher level of live performance. In October 1982, thanks to the devotion of Dr. Demento, he and Molly were flown to California, where Ben appeared at The Country Club, along with fellow musical tummlers Uncle Floyd, whose own vaudevillian TV shows were very much in the Benny Bell milieu, and song parodist "Weird Al" Yankovic, who had just come onto the entertainment scene. Floyd was an admirer of Ben's, and Ben called Floyd his favorite piano accompanist. Their styles were similar, and they became good friends. (When Ben appeared on Uncle Floyd's own television show, he was introduced by the host as "My all-time favorite entertainer.") Yankovic, whose catalog includes such songs as "Eat It," "I Love Rocky Road" and "My Bologna," went on to score 30 Gold and Platinum albums and three Grammy Awards, though that night in Reseda he was still a newcomer.

Demento was more than a fan of Benny Bell's. Like Uncle Floyd, he held quite a bit of affection for Ben and Molly, arranged for all their travel and accommodations, and made sure they were safe, happy and well cared for. Ben and Molly, in turn, were enormously fond of Dr. Demento.

The following year, once again under the auspices of Demento, Ben appeared at the Bottom Line, the famous Greenwich Village cabaret. Then, in 1985 he performed at the Beacon Theatre on upper Broadway. "Weird Al" (now a famous headliner) was on both bills.

The Bottom Line was an intimate club for small, enthusiastic crowds that attracted a diverse list of performers who enjoyed the informality, such as Richie Havens, John Phillips, Henny Youngman, Mart Sahl and others. By contrast, the Beacon, which had first opened during the Roaring 20s, was a 2800-seat, three-tiered showplace that often catered to rock bands such as The Rolling Stones, Aerosmith and Queen.

Ben was a hit at both clubs.

With his advancing age, he felt the need to have a cheat-sheet of lyrics to get him through, though the audiences easily forgave him the professional transgression. They adored him, and he soaked it up. His smiles were endless, as were the smiles on the faces of all the concert-goers in the audience. He still was not a nationwide phenomenon, nor would he ever be—but with plenty of cheering fans making the Country Club, the Bottom Line and the Beacon Theatre shake, rattle and roll with each verse of "Shaving Cream" and each chorus of "Everybody Wants My Fanny," the 79-year-old's resolve to be what he wanted to be, and to do it the way he wanted to do it, was entirely justified.

Once more—seemingly for the thousandth time in his career—there was an extended lull in activity, as far as performing was concerned. Six years passed before he returned to the stage, though the event was quite a spectacular one. Dr. Demento hosted a cable TV show as part of his twentieth anniversary celebration as a professional deejay, and Ben participated along with such popular novelty acts as Bobby Pickett ("Monster Mash"), Tiny Tim ("Tiptoe Through the Tulips"), Sheb Wooley ("The Purple People Eater"), as well as Weird Al Yankovic and his old friend Uncle Floyd, who once again provided Ben with piano accompaniment. At the end of the show, videotaped anniversary cards from Stan Freberg, Cheech Marin, Father Guido Sarducci, George Carlin and several other noted comedians were played to a surprised Dr. Demento.

The show took place at the beautiful, historic Raymond Theatre in Pasadena, California, a 2000-seat music hall that first opened in 1921 and quickly became one of the top vaudeville houses in the country.

Ben was selected to close the show, and he sang what he knew the Demento audience wanted to hear, "Shaving Cream," and nearly the entire house joined in enthusiastically with each chorus. As was by now a staple at all the venues where Dr. Demento, Uncle Floyd and Benny Bell appeared together, Demento and Floyd sang "Shaving Cream" verses of their own, which kept the crowd roaring its approval. The cheers before and after Ben's act were thunderous. It was televised on the Comedy Central cable network.

He had another TV appearance in October 1991 on a show called "Beyond Vaudeville" on Time Warner Cable, which was as impoverished a show as Demento's was opulent. The program worked hard to connect itself with the apparently nonexistent budget. (The credits were hand-scribbled on pieces of scrap paper.) Ben sang "Shaving Cream" and spoke a bit about his early career. His fellow guests included Tiny Tim, tattoo expert Ron Held, Renaissance Man George Kayatta, Mr. Lucky and Stanley the Pig.

Two years later, when he was 87 years old, Ben was asked to appear at Caroline's Comedy Club, the famous night spot in Manhattan where most of the famous comedians of the day appeared to brush up their acts, and newer ones begged to be discovered. The evening was billed as a "Beyond Vaudeville Halloween Spectacular." Comedian Pat Cooper was the emcee, and Ben's fellow acts included nose-whistler Jim Grosso, Dee Nack the Female Elvis, Moses Josiah and his Musical Saw,

Suzanne Muldowney as Spectrum the Ghost King, Joey the Monkey, and Yiddish Fun with Izzy Fertel.

Even into his ninety-first year Ben was still making television appearances, though it was getting harder for him to make the rounds. The old "Beyond Vaudeville" program had been transformed into "Oddville" for MTV, and Ben was a particular favorite of the production team. The studio audiences adored him, as did the other guests. The host, Frank Hope, had remained with the show from its previous version, as did most of the heavily discounted production values—but being on a national and very popular cable network provided a much wider audience than before.

Ben shared the "Oddville" stage with such guests as film director Kevin Smith, actress Joey Lauren Adams, tattooed dancer Clare Ann Matz, human pin cushion Eric Ziobrowski, comedian Steve Belledin, and yet another pig, this one named Wally. Unfortunately, Wally oinked throughout Ben's entire rendition of "The Tattooed Lady."

His mind was still fairly sharp during each performance (he recited most of "Ikey & Mikey" flawlessly by heart), but he was now slowed considerably by his need to use a cane, and his coordination wasn't what it once was: his skilled ukulele playing days were behind him. But his two MTV appearances in 1996 were nonetheless testaments to his endurance and his general outlook, and he fared quite well alongside all the other guests. In fact, sometimes much better.

NEVER FULLY DRESSED

I was ready to take over Manhattan when I was twenty-seven and working on East 43rd Street as a public relations account executive, writing press release after press release for the Minolta camera company. That's not really what I wanted to be doing, but it was a start. Or so I thought. I wanted to believe that public relations could be a stepping stone to becoming a published novelist or produced playwright, and I still believed that Manhattan was mine for the taking.

The problem was, Poppy Benny already owned it.

I guess I already knew that, but it was nice to see it in action in October 1984 when he rented a studio for a few hours at a midtown production facility to shoot one of his video comedy skits. Knowing that I was now working in town, he asked if I wanted to meet him at the studio and play a part in the skit. At 78 my grandfather was still giving his inspirations a good chase all over the city. I remember thinking that I'd feel blessed if at 78 years of age I, too, could do whatever I wanted to do, whenever and wherever I wanted to do it.

I explained to my boss why my lunch hour that day would be a little longer than an hour. Grudgingly, he said okay, and I had to admit to myself that by now boasting about my Benny Bell connection did not have quite the same resonance as it had eight years before, when the "Shaving Cream" revival took New York by storm. Things more or less were back to 'Benny Bell? Who's Benny Bell?'

Poppy Benny held court at the studio with the confidence of an impresario—a George M. Cohan or David Belasco for the 1980s, although with just a few dollars in his pocket. He knew what he wanted and was there to do it exactly that way. The much-younger technicians and assistants at the studio seemed simply to defer to his wishes and desires, regardless of how silly and slapdash the production actually was. After all, my grandfather was both a paying client and a man approaching his eightieth year. He had earned their deference decades ago.

Silly and slapdash it was. The skit, called "The Aqua Syndrome," was in the form of a television talk show. I played the host, Poppy Benny the guest. The 'syndrome' that the guest talked about had something to do with money and marriage, and it was surrounded by vaudevillian punch lines and songs.

I didn't think it was very funny, but neither did Poppy Benny regard my hosting duties as very effective.

Without a live audience—which is what vaudeville really needs to work— the skit seemed strained, out of place and time, and without a vaudevillian personality of my own, I, too, was out of place and time. I could tell that he was frustrated with my more sterile approach to being a host. I didn't want to disappoint him, but there was little I could do about it.

In fact, although I had once been "the kid with the drum" and had been an easy guitar student under his tutelage, I was never really certain how willing he was to accept in me any genuine musical (or musical-comedy) talent beyond what is customary for a grandfather to attribute to a grandson. I know he believed I had some talent—but just how much was the question. With him it was hard to tell. I'll never forget the look on his face when I broke into a Broadway number once, quite unexpectedly. Bonnie and I were newlyweds. We were visiting my parents in Westbury when Grandma Molly and Poppy Benny were there. As a fan of the Broadway musical "Annie," I had memorized the song "You're Never Fully Dressed Without a Smile." In my parents' kitchen that day, someone said something that reminded me of the song—and for some reason I had the urge to croon it right there in front of everyone, in a 1930s style similar to the way the character crooned it in the play. I pulled out all the stops and gave it the full musical-comedy treatment. The look on Poppy Benny's face can only be described as bewildered. Not quite believing, not quite disbelieving. Just bewildered. He had no idea...

Nor did he have any idea what I did in Manhattan as a young professional, which made the situation there even a little more frustrating during the taping of the "Aqua Syndrome." He knew I worked in Manhattan— which is why he invited me to join him at the studio in the first place—but that was about it. He seemed not to wonder what industry I was in or what company I worked for, or even if I had to be back at the office at a certain time. For all his love and devotion, I often questioned how well Poppy Benny really knew me. "You're Never Fully Dressed Without a Smile" and "The Aqua Syndrome" were two of my clues, and I tried not to let that bother me.

The irony, of course, is that had we discussed my job I would have been tempted to bare my soul and admit to him that I really hated doing what I was doing. But that, in turn, would have raised an additional question that I would not have been able to discuss with him at all: did Benny Bell have anything to do with the career choices I had made, and the degrees of risk I may or may not have taken along the way? Should I have relocated to the West Coast after graduating college to try to break into television and motion picture writing? That had once been my plan. Should I have applied for jobs at the media companies in New York or California, instead of public relations agencies, even just to seek a ground floor position as a way of getting my foot in the door? Was there a reason I bounced from one public relations job to another instead of aggressively seeking the profession I truly wanted?

Why didn't I? Unlike Poppy Benny, I tended to trust other people. Unlike Poppy Benny, I wasn't scared of letting the world know who I really was. So what stopped me? Was I too timid? Too scared? Or was I subconsciously taking my parents' advice and doing everything possible not to become another Benny Bell? Perhaps I feared that all the miles I had already logged peddling novels and plays on the sidewalks of New York, and all the finished projects that were sitting in my desk drawers and file cabinets, actually made being a Benny Bell a distinct possibility. So why push it?

Watching Poppy Benny work in that Manhattan studio during "The Aqua Syndrome" taping was a mixed blessing. It was the first and last time we had ever worked together, and sometimes I'm a little sad about that. But I also knew that when the taping was over, he'd go home to Brooklyn and dive head first into some other Benny Bell project, eagerly and undaunted—while I was obligated to go back to 43rd Street to write yet another press release about a Minolta camera.

Don't Worry

In many ways, Benny Bell's career in its final active decade—1986 to 1996—encapsulated all that came before it, and not just the projects themselves, but also the attitudes and approaches that he took on their behalf, from the untiring hucksterism to the paranoid entrepreneurship.

As he had already shown several times in the 1970s, Ben didn't mind at all trying to drum up some show business by tapping into some of the modern fads, and music videos were no exception. MTV had debuted on cable television in 1981, and beginning in 1982 Ben recorded the first of several music-and-comedy videos (including "The Aqua Syndrome"), which he would do throughout the rest of the decade, and which he hoped would be purchased and aired by some of the newer cable networks. "Jingle Time," "Videotunes," "Laugh Along with Benny Bell" and "Voodoo Rock 'n Roll" were among these videos. The productions were low-budget, and it showed. He did, however, manage to have a few of them aired. "Laugh Along with Benny Bell" was shown several times on Manhattan Cable in June 1986, and a short portion of "Voodoo Rock 'n Roll" was shown as part of a news story about Benny Bell in June 1987 on the "News 4 New York" program on WNBC-TV.

There were perhaps better Benny Bell songs that could have been translated into intriguing music videos. "Home Again (Without Pants)," recorded in 1981, comes to mind. In it, a jolly chorus shouts "without pants!" every time Ben describes meeting a member of his family after a long absence. In the hands of a skilled and quirky director, it could have been an outrageous set-up. Even the tender, sanguine "Brooklyn Bridge" might have presented an opportunity for some dramatic story-telling to go along with the tune.

But seeking outside directors was never part of his modus operandi.

Not long after recording "Voodoo Rock 'n Roll," Ben drew up a marketing proposal to present to the Showtime cable-TV network. He thought he might be able to interest the network in a cross-promotion in which bits from the 'spicy jokes and party songs' album he had made in 1977, also called "Showtime," would be played on the air as a way of keeping viewers tuned in. The album was full of little music-and-comedy quickies, and the only real connection to the cable network was the name Showtime. Network management politely refused his proposal. He made similar proposals to other entertainment companies, as well as to performers such as Joan Rivers who, in January 1984, sent him a letter thanking him for his suggestion:

"I was indeed a fan of 'Pincus the Peddler' and delighted to know that you wrote those songs," she said in her note. "Thank you for suggesting that I sing, but if you heard my voice, you'd know why I am a comedienne. However, I wish you the best of luck. Most sincerely, Joan Rivers."

(He wrote to Rivers once again nine years later, as the run of her live syndicated talk show was coming to an end. In that letter he reit-erated the popularity of "Shaving Cream," and suggested that "your studio audiences will sing along if you are kind enough to give me a spotlight on one of your closing TV shows—and you may donate my fee to charity." There is no record of a response.)

Meanwhile, he continued dabbling with short video productions for the next few years—mostly simple visualizations of jokes and word-plays. As with the Showtime proposal, he hoped that somewhere in the burgeoning cable TV market would be a forward-thinking executive who would embrace his vaudevillian video skits and use them as breaks between programs. One of the last he produced was called "Don't Worry! Here is How," a two-minute comic monologue about the wisdom of refusing to dwell on negative thoughts. It never aired.

But that didn't stop Ben from believing that some of his material was so original and engaging that other professionals might even want to use it from time to time, without his consent.

As a case in point, in 1990 he went to see the juvenile motion picture, "Teenage Mutant Ninja Turtles," because he thought that one of his old songs had been borrowed. In 1963 he had written, copyrighted and recorded a curious ditty called "The Turtle Song," which was a sort of fictional club-set-to-music, and upon hearing about the new Ninja Turtle movie, he thought the possibility existed that one of its creators knew of his 27-year-old song and commandeered its concept and maybe even its music and lyrics. He certainly had no interest in the story, the genre, the special effects or the popular animated TV show on which the movie was based. But he *had* to find out if his song had been used.

Of course that wasn't the case, but he had to suffer through 93 minutes of raucous comic cartoon warfare to come to that conclusion.

BREEZING THROUGH

*T*he death of a loved one, in addition to being heartrending and irrevo-
cable, can also be very scary. You never know what you're going to find
when you start to go through the odds and ends they left behind.

Certainly I was already aware of much of what made Poppy Benny
Poppy Benny. Knowing about his compulsions, paranoia and vast assortment
of projects and strategies, it was never much of a surprise to find a few real
oddities among the odds and ends—something that would remind me all over
again just how distinctive and eccentric a personality he was. I'd like to think
that if he had a little more focus, patience and a willingness to trust other professionals, some of those eccentricities might have made him a very rich man.

The Playbill from "Fiddler on the Roof" is one of odder things I found.
Had I not decided to flip through page by page, I may have tossed it aside
as merely a souvenir of the popular Broadway show that he saw in the mid
1960s. Inside the Playbill he had jotted down, in pencil, probably while watching the show, a comprehensive account of how long each scene ran, which
instruments were used to orchestrate various storylines, and other notations.
"Fiddler on the Roof" was, at that time, one of the most successful musicals
in Broadway history, and apparently he wanted to try to reach the same
zenith of success with a show of his own, and he turned that Playbill into an
instruction manual to make it happen.

Whether or not he ever began his own 'Fiddler' is unknown. But that he wanted to, and probably believed from the bottom of his heart that he could, is clear.

And then there was the fart record.

Benny Bell albums and singles weren't the only ones in his personal collection. He had many by Al Jolson and other Tin Pan Alley crooners, plus a few sound effects records. And he also had a 33⅓ rpm record (on a 10-inch disc) in a plain white album cover with nothing on it but the handwritten words "Fart Contest."

Research shows that it was recorded in the mid-1940s purportedly by the staff of the Canadian Broadcast Corporation. The record's official title was "The Crepitation Contest," and on it, sportscaster Sidney Brown narrates a flatulence match between Lord Windismere and Paul Boomer. Brown also interviews both contestants. Apparently the record was never commercially sold, but used as a gag gift by certain individuals and then put into the underground distribution network by habitual collectors. The originators used the names of different production companies (probably all fake) on various copies of the disk, such as Laff Records and Humor Records. The one my grandfather had was listed as being produced by Breeze Records.

He may have purchased "The Crepitation Contest" to have some new sound effects at his disposal, though I don't recall ever hearing flatulence on any Benny Bell record. Maybe he just wanted to see what other people were doing in the world of novelty recordings—and to think about how he could do a better job.

THE OTHER SIDE

Grandma Molly was my third grandparent to pass away, but the first I had seen so close to death.

In July 1994 she was admitted to Coney Island Hospital suffering from emphysema (she had smoked her entire adult life; Ben never did). I took Bonnie and the children to visit her as soon as we had heard. Bonnie seemed to know that death was imminent. She saw it in Grandma Molly's eyes and could barely contain herself. She had to leave the room several times to cry.

I knew it was common for one's mind to go in new directions when it sensed the end was near, but I had never really seen it happen. Until then. Grandma Molly started to tell my children the story of Adam and Eve. I don't recall what, if anything, triggered it, but I do know that of all the stories she told throughout the years, the one about Adam and Eve had never been one of them. Also, despite her painful wheezing, her dry, sunken eyes, and her white, withered skin, she told the story in as graceful, sincere and serene a manner as anyone has ever told it.

The next day she died.

Ben was lost. His partner and protector for life was gone. At her funeral he wept like a baby. He waved his hands in big, childlike gestures and wailed, "Bye, bye, Molly. Bye, bye."

It was the first real emotion I ever saw from him.

At the cemetery, slowly returning to a semblance of form, he looked at the plot in which her casket would be lowered, then looked at the one next to it that was reserved for him, and quipped,

"For 67 years I slept on her right. Soon I'll have to sleep on her left."

The next five years was just a matter of surviving. While he did make a few final television appearances to sing the old songs, there were no more new records, no more books, no more marketing gimmicks. Ben just had to try to stay focused enough not to trip and fall or get lost on East 16th Street. I visited him several times at his apartment during that period. He was usually in an undershirt and wrinkled pants, and unshaven. I combined one of my visits with a meeting I had in another part of Brooklyn with a literary agent. How I would have loved to talk about my meeting, but I had no reason to believe that he'd be able to appreciate my excitement. When I arrived at the apartment, he kissed me. That was something new. Maybe things *had* changed. Maybe with Molly gone he suddenly realized we're all mortal and may need more of an intimate connection than the kind he had time for in the past. We did talk about the meeting—but just a very little bit. His favorite expression for the last few years had been, "I have a memory like a fish," and it was starting to manifest itself. It was difficult to hold a conversation.

Before too long my father and uncle determined he would be better off in a nursing home. The apartment was too messy, the stairs to the street too demanding. Self-sufficiency was being lost daily. I entertained dreams of seeing him reside at the Actor's Home in Englewood, New Jersey, where there were vaudevillians and Borscht Belters aplenty. I researched it, but the cost was prohibitive and the waiting list long, so a facility in Queens was selected instead. On one hand it may have been a better idea, for who knows how he would have fared in the presence of so many showbiz veterans who probably had massive egos of their own and may have known one or more of the people who had rejected his projects or cheated him out of money. On the other hand, the place in which he ended up had very little dignity—and every decent elderly person is entitled to some dignity. It was a dark and dingy facility, and often smelled of urine. There was some evidence that one of the workers there rang up high bills on Ben's phone and stole his candy.

He mistrusted everyone there and fretted constantly about the health and whereabouts of his two sons, as if they were youngsters at sleep away camp. Perhaps in his mind they were. There was little laughter in those final weeks, and very few smiles. Benny Bell was already dead. Benjamin Samberg was dying.

My parents and I tried to entice management at the nursing home to make some improvements, and on my own I continued to research other places, but it was all for naught. He died on July 6, 1999 and was interred at New Montefiore Cemetery on Long Island, where he is now resting on his beloved's left side, and probably laughing and smiling again.

FINAL NOTES

*B*enjamin Samberg's professional life could best be described as being *firmly established—for 70 years—on the outer fringes of show business. Thousands of people knew who he was, but millions didn't. He wrote hundreds of songs and produced more than a hundred of records, but his name will never be listed in any published account of American popular music. He appeared on television several times, though the market reach was often very small and his fellow guests were frequently very strange. He was a natural and joyful entertainer who felt entirely at home on stage, but live performances over the course of his career numbered only a few, and often as just one act among many others on the same bill.*

Still, at times he came so close to broad popularity that he was able to sense what stardom was like, although he was always so far away from it that he could never depend on his celebrity for the next rent check.

What must it have been like to be on the fringe like that? It has driven others to distraction. Perhaps my mother and father didn't want me to be another Benny Bell not just because of the possibility of being driven to distraction (although that's certainly part of it), but because of the personal qualities sometimes needed to be driven there. They didn't want me to be paranoid, suspicious, hasty, bigheaded and pigheaded.

I guess they were just being parents.

My grandfather had many talents—some of which went virtually unexplored—which may have made his fringe standing a little harder to swallow from time to time. A few of his uncultivated gifts showed up in some recordings that required him to let out a little more personality and emotion than in others. In a number such as "Down by the Old Mill Stream" (written by Tell Taylor in 1910 but given a slight novelty twist in Ben's recorded version), he showed he had the chops of a skilled scat vocalist. In "Pincus the Peddler," his voice took on a decidedly melancholy cant, without losing the character's sense of wonder and optimism. Some of his arrangements were quite sophisticated. The stories he told out loud completely eliminated the line between truth and imagination, which made them all the more appealing. He was a gifted raconteur.

Mostly, though, he stuck to silly songs, vaudevillian skits and curious marketing gimmicks. And he did it all on his own. Which proves that as much as he did, he didn't do enough. He should have made a serious study of what worked best for him, and should have given those things the same effort he gave everything else. And he should have let other people help him. But that's not the vision he had for himself as an entertainer, and so he never even considered other options, or any other advice.

He claimed in a handful of interviews that he had always supported himself and his family with music. That wasn't entirely true. He had many jobs over the years and accepted many loans. But if one were to measure the number of days, weeks and months he devoted to music against the number of days, weeks and months in which he delivered packages, ran errands or manned a pushcart, there would hardly be a contest. Music would win every time. So he can easily be forgiven his little white lie. Besides, his sense of pride in making such a statement ran so deep that to not forgive it would be unforgivable.

In addition to being an entertainer, he was a loving, caring and devoted husband and father. As a grandfather he was both larger than life and accessible at the same time. It probably would have been easy for me to enjoy him as a grandfather even if he hadn't been Benny Bell, the novelty songwriter and singer. It was the personality that counted—the nuttiness, the storytelling, the silly asides—which, perhaps, actually meant that Benny Bell was the personality and the personality was Benny Bell. In any event, I certainly wouldn't have wanted an Irving Berlin for a grandfather, who was a virtual stranger to his own grandchildren, having driven them away (along with other members of his family) with his spells of anger and the cold, ruthless quality of his character.

Shortly after Poppy Benny died, my father was sitting in the den of his house one Saturday night watching a rerun of "The Lawrence Welk Show" on TV, the program my grandfather loved. As the smiling honky-tonk pianist Jo Ann Castle was being introduced by the legendary host, the phone rang. My father glanced at my mother, an incredulous look on both their faces. Poppy Benny always used to call when Jo Ann Castle was about to take the stage. So my father went to the kitchen and picked up the receiver. No one was on the other end. He just smiled, shook his head, hung up the phone and went back to watch the rest of the show.

It was the perfect little ironic topper to a perfectly acceptable relationship between the two of them. Had my father been more of a selfish and reactionary man, I'm certain he would have looked back on his childhood with anger, recalling his father's stubbornness and mistrust, which could be at least partially blamed for the near-poverty in which the family found itself for much of the 1930s and more than half of the 1940s. But my father was wiser and more composed than someone else might have been from that background, and I tend to think that his entire life-view of his father was similar to his reaction when the phone rang during Jo Ann Castle's introduction: a simple smile and a curious shake of his head.

On the other hand, how is it possible to sum up a life as full as my grandfather's with just a smile and a shake of the head? Maybe others can, but not me: I'm the one who went through an entire file cabinet of personal papers that painted quite a remarkable portrait of a man obsessed with ideas and notions and endeavors and plans and possibilities. Going through his notebooks and ledgers, one could easily conclude that it was Benjamin Samberg, not George Burns or James Brown or anyone else, who was the hardest working man in show business. And that's a trait I wouldn't have minded inheriting, regardless of how my parents felt about it.

Poppy Benny created so many lists that it's amazing he found time to write any songs at all, let alone record, promote and perform them. Of course, his penchant for keeping lists and reference notes was so encompassing that it seems to have bordered on the obsessive and the compulsive, and that could have been another small crack in the overall foundation. There are no less than five separate books listing more than 600 original songs, most of them repeated from one book to another. There is one that includes the names of record companies, copyright statistics and other musically-related information. Another lists relatives, trust funds, residences, social security numbers of family members, names of deceased friends, and dozens of other personal inventories.

A journal he kept between 1919 and 1965 includes a family history, insurance policies, memorial dates, schools attended and, of course, more lists of songs.

He kept little notebooks with such data as the names of companies that provided goods and services that he may have wanted to use some day for one project or another (animation studios, cartoon libraries), as well as newspaper columnists, advertising agencies, magazine publishers and much more. He kept copies of display ads, some of which he was interested in for himself, such as Songwriters Wanted, Ballads Wanted and Surplus Albums Wanted, and others that he collected as sources of humor for future skits and songs.

As I was reviewing these pieces of his life I realized that there are many other similarities between the two of us beyond his "Hobo's Union" booklet and my "Homeless Equity" play. That was just the beginning. I glimpsed dozens of projects, plans, ideas and even working methods that are remarkably parallel to many of my own. I even discovered a list of titles for songs he had not yet composed, which was an eerie reminder of the list I keep in my office of the dozens of plays, books and movies I intend to write one day. Revelations like that can be uncanny and mystifying, yet they also provide the strongest evidence we have that life isn't all a random series of choices, but that sometimes there's a little predetermination built into who we are, how we are, and why we want to do what we want to do.

But there are significant differences between us, as well.

For one thing, my grandfather never wore his professional frustrations and disappointments on his sleeve, knowing there was little value in that. But I have, allowing my wife, children, parents, friends and coworkers to see, far too often, how discouraged I've been more times than I care to remember about various literary and theatrical pursuits that haven't panned out. Also, my grandfather never let a professional road take him too far from where he wanted to be. He would never let that happen. I have. For more than a quarter of a century I accepted a series of corporate positions that barely provided any professional satisfaction at all—jobs that often took me farther and farther away, professionally speaking, from where I really wanted to be.

Why did I? Did the career of Benny Bell have anything to do with that?

If so, should I blame him, or take responsibility for my own actions? Or inactions, as the case may be.

Benny Bell never let out more than just one of the thousand clowns that were hiding inside of him. The Ben everyone knew was the only Ben he wanted them to know—indeed, it was the only one that he permitted to exist. That, of course, is not always a good thing. It can be very limiting in more ways than one. But on the other hand, he never became one of the millions of clowns out there who compromised their visions out of hopelessness, anxiety, failure or any of the other interruptions of life that make many people concede to alternate plans. He had no alternate plan. Poppy Benny really had just one career throughout his entire life and, despite the financial strife and relative obscurity that tagged along, it was the only one he really wanted.

Which is why to me he was the most successful entertainer who ever lived.

The End

Appendix I

LYRICS TO SELECTED BENNY BELL SONGS

The Automobile Song

A couple once was seated

In a little motor car

They were holding hands together

As the motor loudly roared

And the price of gas went up to sixty-two.

He was an automobile mechanic

Working steady throughout the year

And in terms of his profession

He whispered in her ear...

Will you love me when my carburetor's busted

Will you love me when I cannot shift my gears

When my spark plug is as dead as Kelsey's doorknob

As my clutch begins to slip will you shed tears?

Will you love me when my old exhaust gets noisy

Will you love me when my pump is on the blink

Oh, heck

When my fender has a dent

And my piston rod is bent

Will you love me when my flivver is a wreck?

Will you love me when my fuel pipe is empty

Will you move me when my rear end's worn and torn

Will you love me when my rim rod's old and rusty

Will you love me when I cannot blow my horn?

Will you love me when my inner tube is busted

Will you love me when my tank begins to leak

Oh, heck

When the junkman says "No use"

And my nuts and bolts are loose

Will you love me when my flivver is a wreck?

The Bowery Bums

I've slept on the stations

I've slept on the rails

On tables, in stables and forty old jails

I've slept on a mountain

I've slept in a trench

But the place I love best is the part on a bench.

Chiri bim bim bum bam

What a big bum I am

I want you to know

I'm the best hobo man.

They've thrown me from boxcars

They've thrown me from barns
From house tops, from barrooms
From hotels and farms
They've thrown me in snowstorms
In downpours of hail
But the worse was the time I was thrown into jail.

Chiri bim bim bum bam
What a big bum I am
I want you to know
I'm the best hobo man

Brooklyn Bridge
Oh boy, what a day
Oh joy, I feel so gay.

Hey, Brooklyn Bridge
I'm thankful as can be
You found my girl for me
The world is now sublime
And everything is fine.

Oh, Brooklyn Bridge
My honey ran away
But now she's back to stay
Because of you

Her car broke down with a flat
I came along

Took care of that
And then till dawn we stayed up
Kissed and made up.

Brooklyn Bridge
With all those stars above
You helped us fall in love
We're sweethearts again.

Everybody Wants My Fanny

Everyone is out to get my Fanny
Everybody wants to see my Fanny
Everybody likes to hold my Fanny
But she loves no one but me.

Everybody wants to seize my Fanny
Everybody likes to squeeze my Fanny
They do everything to please my Fanny
Still she loves no one but me.

Oh, don't touch my Fanny
Please don't ever try
My little Fanny is reserved
For just one guy.

That's why I
Never let another love light blind me
Everywhere I go you'll always find me

With my little Fanny right behind me

'Cause she's so in love with me

Everyone who ever spied my Fanny

Tried to hang around beside my Fanny

Maybe I should go and hide my Fanny

Or she'll find somebody new.

I've seen lots of Fannys in my time

And frequently their cheeks were close to mine

But never have I held one so divine

Like the Fanny that belongs to me.

We will be married

Some day next June

And when we go away

To spend our honeymoon,

I know that

Everyone is gonna miss my Fanny

No one ever could resist my Fanny

But they wouldn't dare to kiss my Fanny

'Cause she's so in love with me.

Go to Work, You Jerk

If you wanna have lots of cash

If you wanna have bills to flash

Go to work, you jerk, stop hanging around

If you wanna wear fancy clothes
If you wanna see Broadway shows
Go to work, you jerk, stop hanging around

Nobody likes a lazy guy who's always broke
And believe me, it's no joke
It makes you hazy, crazy.

If you wanna be bright and gay
If you like three meals a day
Go to work, you jerk, stop hanging around.

A Goose for My Girl

I used to worry when Thanksgiving day was near
What can I give my girl to fill her heart with cheer
But I solved that problem, I'm a clever boy
I know exactly how to fill her heart with joy.

I'm gonna give my girl a goose for Thanksgiving
It won't surprise her since I did it once before
She jumps just like the deuce
Every time she gets a goose
Perhaps I ought to give her two or more.

I wish I could afford to buy her a turkey
But turkeys cost so much and I'm our of work, you see
So I'll just give my girl a goose
A good old-fashioned goose
I wish someone would do the same for me.

I'm gonna give my girl a goose for Thanksgiving
My friends all tell me that the plan is very smart
In fact, her daddy said to me
Very confidentially
That's just the way he won her mama's heart.

So if you want to make your darling feel happy
Then take a tip from me and do the same thing, too
Go on and give your girl a goose
A nice, soft, tender goose
And you'll discover if her love is true.

I don't mean gander
A good old-fashioned goose will do

Grandpa Had a Long One

My grandpa had a long one
It nearly touched his chin
My uncle has a small one
With hardly any skin
My daddy has a broad one
Just like a rolling pin
But mine is big and round and fat
It looks more like a baseball bat
You never saw a nose like mine before.

Noses, noses, they run in my family
Some are big, some are small

Some you cannot see at all
Noses, noses, for over a century
Now, isn't it a shame
There are no two the same.

My cousin has a bent one
It really is a pip
My nephew has a short one
With freckles on the tip
His stepson has a thin one
Just like a horse's whip
But mine, I tell you, beats the band
My sweetie thinks it's simply grand
You never saw a nose like mine before.

My brother has a big one
That's always in his way
His junior has a hard one
Just like a hunk of clay
My uncle has a cold one
That leaks all through the day
But mine's a peach, I tell you guys
It really ought to win a prize
You never saw a nose like mine before.

Home Again (Without Pants)

I'm going home again (without pants)
Where I can roam again (without pants)
How happy I will be (without pants)
To see my family (without pants)
I've been away a long, long time
And every night I pine
To be back in that neighborhood
With all those friends of mine.

I'll meet my brother Jim (without pants)
I always picture him (without pants)
I'll see my sister Claire (without pants)
I know that she'll be there (without pants)
A lot of guys might not agree
But take a tip from me
There's no place like home sweet home.

Ikey & Mikey

Ikey and Mikey
Were digging in a well
Said Ikey to Mikey
'I hope you go to
Helen's birthday party
You will be quite a hit'
Said Mikey to Ikey
'I think you're full of
Shi-sh-ke-bab and pizza

And you drink a lot of tea
And every hour on the hour
You have to make a
Peanut butter sandwich
To feed your hungry heart
But when you eat those Boston beans
You always leave a
Foreign letter in my mailbox
You're a crazy man
Sometimes I get so angry
I could kick you in the
Candy store and hold your head
Beneath the water tap
'Cause when you say you're sorry
That's just a load of
Crabgrass, my buddy
So if you're really wise
You'll ask me no more questions
And I'll tell you no more lies'

Ikey and Mikey
Once had a luncheon date
They paid the man a quarter
For a doughnut on a plate
The waiter said 'Your quarter
Has a hole through and through'
So Ikey told the waiter
'Your doughnut has one too'

Now, Ikey and Mikey
Are known from coast to coast
And everybody drinks up
When they hear their famous toast
'The morning sun may kiss the grass
The clock may kiss the hours that pass
The flowing wine can kiss the glass
And you, my friend
Drink hearty!

Jack of all Trades

I used to work in Toledo
In a department store
I used to work in Toledo
I did, but I don't anymore
A lady came in for some candy
We had it in the store
Kisses she wanted, kisses she got
That's why I'm not there anymore.

I used to work in New Haven
In a department store
I used to work in New Haven
I did, but I don't anymore
A lady came in with a can for gas
We sold it in the store
I whispered, 'Ma'am, you've got some can'
That's why I'm not there anymore.

I used to work in Milwaukee
In a department store
I used to work in Milwaukee
I did, but I don't anymore
A lady came in to our butcher shop
We had one in the store
A goose she wanted, a goose she got
That's why I'm not there anymore.

I used to work in Waukegan
In a department store
I used to work in Waukegan
I did, but I don't anymore
A lady came in for a pinch of salt
We had some in the store
A pinch she wanted, a pinch she got
That's why I'm not there anymore.

I used to work on Long Island
In a department store
I used to work on Long Island
I did, but I don't anymore
A lady came in for a felt hat
We had them in the store
Felt she wanted, felt she got
That's why I'm not there anymore.

My Condominium

It cost me a lot, it's a very lovely spot
And I'm proud of what I've got—my condominium
For people who care there is romance in the air
You can find it everywhere in a condominium
A great social plan, but you must grab what you can
There's seven widows to each man, that's the minimum
And my children so dear call me once every year
They are glad that they stuck me here in a condominium.

No doggie, no pup, aggravation fills my cup
When the maintenance goes up in my condominium
It's really a crime how the taxes seem to climb
They keep rising all the time in my condominium
The neighbors you meet put on airs that can't be beat
Though they came from Hester Street
Where they smelled from cinnamon
At recreation, of course, you can't help feeling cross
Everybody is a boss in a condominium.

They all take a chance with a group that swing and dance
Many seniors lose their pants in a condominium
They go into a rage like a tiger in a cage
If you ever tell their age in a condominium
When you're feeling fine everything is just sublime
Life could be a real good time—that's my opinium
But I declare over there if you need a doctor's care
You gotta be a millionaire in a condominium.

My Janitor's Can

There's a good-natured janitor I used to know
When I lived in a tenement house long ago
To watch children play was her life's great desire
But she was afraid they would start a fire
And all throughout the day she'd lecture the children and say,

I don't care if you play on the sidewalk
I don't mind if you dance in the hall
You may even play ball on the staircase
Or with chalk scratch your name on the wall
I don't care if you ransack the basement
If you're happy then I'm happy too
But don't stick a burning cigar in my can
("I won't tolerate it!")
That's all that I ask of you.

I don't care if you smash out a window
I don't mind if you slide down the rail
I don't care if you play with my pussy
Just as long as you don't pull her tail
I don't care if you pull out the molding
I'll forgive everything that you do,
But don't stick a burning cigar in my can
("You want to start a fire?")
That's all that I ask of you.

One Dollar

I took my girl to a fancy dance
In a million dollar hall
The place was grand was a big brass band
But they served no food at all
And so we went to a restaurant
Where the highbrows congregate
She said she wasn't hungry, but this is what she ate.

A lamb chop raw, a plate of slaw
A chicken and a roast
A jumbo course of applesauce
And a soft shelled crab on toast
A big beef stew, a lobster, too
I began to wipe my collar
When she called for pie I thought I'd die
For I only had one dollar.

She said, "Oh, Joe, just before we go
I would like to drink a toast."
I never saw such a toast before
Anywhere from coast to coast.
I soon found out that without a doubt
She must have an extra tank
She said she wasn't thirsty, but this is what she drank.

A whiskey downed, a highball round
That made me shake with fear
A ginger pop with cubes on top

And a schooner filled with beer
A glass of ale, a gin cocktail
I was on the verge to holler
When she asked for more I hit the floor
For I only had one dollar.

My face was mild but my heart ran wild
Everyone could hear me sigh
I was a wreck when I saw the check
With the bouncer standing by I said,
'Now Bo, I ain't got no dough
And the joke is all on you.'
He took me by the collar, and here's what I went through.

He tore my clothes, he bust my nose
He hit me with a pail
He spun me high, then let me fly
And you should've seen me sail
I had no doubt I'd land way, way out
In the town of Walla Walla.
Take a tip, old pal, don't meet this gal
When you only have one dollar.

Pincus the Peddler

I'm Pincus the Peddler
A broken-hearted peddler
The most unlucky fella that was ever born
My mama in Slobodka
Was drinking too much vodka
And left me stranded on a Sunday morn.

My papa was a plumber
Who doubled as a drummer
I never really saw the fella wear a frown
His whiskers were the longest
The toughest and the strongest
How well they used to keep his pants from falling down.

Oh hacha-charn-i-ay
Oh Californ-i-ay
Oh Pennsylvan-i-ay
I'm Pincus the Peddler, Brooklyn U.S.A.

I didn't want to struggle
So I planned a way to smuggle
My papa and myself into the U.S.A.
We knew just how to do it
And so before we knew it
We landed in Canarsie on a stormy day.

But soon I met a woman
A dirty, rotten woman
At first she made me happy then she made me blue

Instead of gaining knowledge
But sending me to college
She sent me to the races and they cleaned me through.

Oh hacha-charn-i-ay
Oh Mississip-i-ay
Oh Albuquerqu-i-ay
I'm Pincus the Peddler, Brooklyn U.S.A.

"Twas at a game of rummy
She called me a dummy
I punched her in the mouth because that makes me mad
She lifted her umbrella
So I kicked her down the cellar
And broke the nicest girdle that she ever had.

She went to Ellis Island
To send me back to my land
The things she told the people there were very bad
I never thought they'd do it
And yet, before I knew it
They packed my trunk and sent me back to Petrograd.

Oh hacha-charn-i-ay
Good old Jamaica Bay
Hooray for Rockaway
I'm Pincus—but no more in the U.S.A.

Shaving Cream

I have a sad story to yell you
It may hurt your feelings a bit
Last night as I walked into my bathroom
I stepped in a big pile of...

Shaving cream, be nice and clean
Shave every day and you'll always look keen.

I think I'll break off with my girlfriend
Her antics are queer, I'll admit
Each time I say, 'Darling, I love you"
She tells me that I'm full of...

Shaving cream, be nice and clean
Shave every day and you'll always look keen.

Our baby fell out of the window
You'd think that her head would be split
But good luck was with her that morning
She fell in a barrel of...

Shaving cream, be nice and clean
Shave every day and you'll always look keen.

My old lady died in a bathtub
She died from a terrible fit
In order to fulfill her wishes
She was buried in six feet of...

Shaving cream, be nice and clean

Shave every day and you'll always look keen.

When I was in France with the army
One day I looked into my kit
I thought I would find me a sandwich
But the darn thing was loaded with...

Shaving cream, be nice and clean
Shave every day and you'll always look keen.

And now, folks, my story has ended
I think it is time I should quit
If any of you feel offended
Stick your head in a bucket of...

Shaving cream, be nice and clean
Shave every day and you'll always look keen.

She Got Her Tid-Bit

She got her tid-bit and now she's happy
She got her tid-bit and now she's gay
I never thought caviar could mean so much to her
Why, she'd rather eat her caviar than wear a color fur
And now she's happy, I'll say she's happy
Her boyfriend tells the world her eyes are all aglow
For since that sweet kid got her tid-bit
She's the happiest girl that I know

She's Still Got It

See that girlie over there
I'd like to break her jaw
Every day in every way
I hate her more and more
She's got something I want bad
And try so hard to get
She promised me a hundred times
But I ain't seen it yet.

She's still got it
She's still got it
I don't know who she's saving it for
I still want it
She won't give it
I'll tell the world it's making me sore.

The way that gal is treating me
Is really just a crime.
I come each night but she postpones it
For another time

And she's still got it
She's still got it
I hope she let's me have it some day.

You may be wondering what she has
That makes me feel this way
I lent her a library book
That I must return today

But she's still got it
She's still got it
I think I'll never see it again.

Ship Ahoy, Sailor Boy

One night while strolling merrily
A sailor said hello to me
I walked away like a good girl should
But he followed me as I knew he would.

He said he's sure we'd met before
I'm just the girl he's looking for
I said, "Go 'way" like a good girl should
But he hung around as I knew he would

Ship ahoy, sailor boy
On the briny sea
Ship ahoy, sailor boy
But come home safe to me.

Our conversation was sublime
But when the clock struck half past nine
I said good night like a good girl should
But he took me home as I knew he would.

He kissed me once, he kissed me twice
And though it seemed like paradise
I ran upstairs like a good girl should
But he followed me like I knew he would.

Ship ahoy, sailor boy
On the briny sea
Ship ahoy, sailor boy
But come home safe to me.

Six Feet Under

Where will we be in a hundred years from now?
Let me tell you:

Six feet under, safe and sound
Green grass growing all around
The more you worry, I declare
The sooner you'll be planted there.

Ever since the world began
Money's been a curse on man
Work and slave and earn and spend
Where does it get you in the end?

Six feet under, safe and sound
Green grass growing all around
The more you worry, I declare
The sooner you'll be planted there.

Hurry, hurry, night and day
Rush rush rush your life away
Late to bed and late to dine
But you'll soon have lots of time.

Six feet under, safe and sound
Green grass growing all around
The more you worry, I declare
The sooner you'll be planted there.

One guy marches off to war
Comes back stronger than before
Then he walks across the street
Bingo, and he's fast asleep.

Six feet under, safe and sound
Green grass growing all around
The more you worry, I declare
The sooner you'll be planted there.

Rich man, poor man, beggar, bum
Some have money, some have none
But the score is always tied
When they're resting side by side.

Six feet under, safe and sound
Green grass growing all around
The more you worry, I declare
The sooner you'll be planted there.

Sweet Violets

When I was a handsome young fellow
I sure had the time of my life
But one day a man broke my backbone
When I ran away with his...

Sweet violets
Sweeter than all the roses
Covered all over from head to foot
Covered all over with snow.

Once day I forgot my suspenders
And took my girl out to a dance
While dancing I heard someone holler,
"Hey, mister, you're losing your...

Sweet violets
Sweeter than all the roses
Covered all over from head to foot
Covered all over with snow.

I once took a shave and a haircut
The barber was drunk, goodness knows
He took out a big brand new razor
And he cut off the tip of my...

Sweet violets
Sweeter than all the roses
Covered all over from head to foot
Covered all over with snow.

Take a Ship for Yourself

Every time we take a trip
You always get my goat
I like trains and buses
But you like a ferry boat
Well, the next time we go traveling
Ships are out and I declare
You go your way, I'll go mine
And I'll meet you over there.

You take a ship for yourself
I'll take a train by myself
If you can't fly in planes
Or ride in buses or in trains
Then go take a ship for yourself.

Take a battleship, an excursion ship
Or a fishing ship will do
And if you can't take a big ship
Then take a small canoe.

Bon voyage to you, my friend
I'll meet you at the journey's end
If you like the briny seas
The rolling waves, an ocean breeze
Then go take a ship for yourself

The Tattooed Lady

Oh, listen to my story, boys, I need your sympathy
And to prove her love is sweet as sugar cane toddy
She had my picture tattooed on her body

She has the landing of the Pilgrims on her shoulder
And on her back she has the sunset in the West
And beside her dimpled knees
She has two great big apple trees
And the pyramids look real upon her chest.

When she decided that she'd like to add my picture
She simply could not find a vacant spot, you see
So she tattooed my poor face in a most peculiar place
Now, whenever she sits down she sits on me.

She has a small gardenia tattooed on her elbow
And on her hip she has a lovely Queen of May
And underneath her shapely spine, if you look close, pal of mine
You'll see the Mississippi River all the way.

She has a rusty hinge that's tattooed on her kneecap
It looks so real it squeaks each time she bends her knee
But she filled me with disgrace when she added my poor face
For whenever she sits down she sits on me.

Now do you wonder why I look so sad and worried
And do you wonder why my head is bending low
Sometimes I'd like to take a chance and give her a swift kick in the pants
But if I do I'd only kick myself, I know.

The only time that anyone can see my picture
Is when the tattooed lady takes a bath, oh gee
I get black and blue, of course
Every time she rides a horse
'Cause whenever she sits down she sits on me.

Valentine Polka

I'm crazy over Daisy
I'm woozy over Susie
I'm batty over Hattie
So who's gonna be my valentine?

I'm silly over Lillie
I'm fussy over Gussie
I'm loony over Junie
So who's gonna be my valentine?

Nina is a lovely girl
Tina sets my head awhirl
Lena is a precious pearl
What a cruel dilemma
Ray is simply heavenly
May is sweet as she can be
Fay is always nice to me
So is Flo and Emma.

I think the world of Stella
I'd like to be her fella
I hate to give up Bella
So who's gonna be my valentine?

Wading in the Water

She went wading in the water
And she got her feet wet
Wading in the water
And she got her toes wet
She went wading in the water
And she got her ankles wet
But she didn't get her (clap, clap) wet
Yet.

She went a little deeper
And she got her legs wet
She went a little deeper
And she got her calves wet
She went a little deeper
And she got her knees wet
But she didn't get her (clap clap) wet
Yet.

She went wading in the water
And she got her hands wet
Wading in the water
And she got her wrists wet

She went wading in the water
And she got her hips wet
But she didn't get her (clap clap) wet
Yet.

She went a little deeper
And she got her elbows wet
She went a little deeper
And she got her shoulders wet
She went a little deeper
And she got her neck wet
But she didn't get her (clap clap) wet
Yet.

Wading in the water
Wading in the water
And she finally got her face all wet.

BENNY BELL DISCOGRAPHY

*T*he following list includes most of Ben Samberg's 33, 45 and 78 rpm records that are known to have been recorded for commercial distribution, and that to a great degree are still available in collections across the country. A handful of individual songs that are known by fans but not listed here have been excluded because of inconclusive evidence about their original market availability on recorded discs and, mostly in the case of the 78s, the likelihood that loss, breakage and their original scarcity have rendered them largely unavailable today. It must also be noted that Ben issued many records numerous times coupled with different tracks on the other side, and that he also reissued several songs as recording technology evolved from one format to another, all of which somewhat complicates the complete accuracy of the discography.

All recordings were written and performed by Ben Samberg (most often as Benny Bell or one of the other pseudonyms), except where otherwise noted.

33⅓ rpm Albums
Be a Comedian (Enterprise)
Cocktail Party Songs (Madison)
Comic Opera (Madison)
Crazy Songs (Madison)
The Face on the Bar-Room Floor (Enterprise)

If You Can't Come, Call Up (Cocktail Novelty)
Jewish American (Enterprise)
Kosher Comedy (Madison)
Laugh Along with Pincus (Madison)
Long Playing Jewish Comedy, Parts I and II (Bell)
Long Playing Jewish Comedy, Parts III and IV (Bell)
Novelty Time (Embassy)
Pincus the Peddler (Enterprise)
Shaving Cream (Vanguard)
Showtime: In Your Own Living Room (Madison)
To the Bride: G'Zint Mit Parnussa (Zion)

45 rpm Records (*side B in italics*)

Aspirin Tablets, *Yum Yum Yum* (Madison)
Baby Cohen's Bris, *Dark Eyes in a Jam* (Madison)
Baseball Jamboree [The Wildcats—instrumental], *Dark Eyes in a Jam* [The Wildcats—instrumental] (Madison)
Baloney, *Who's Gonna Be My Valentine* (Enterprise)
Bygones [vocal by Mister X], *The Wedding Waltz* [Mister X] (Madison)
The Carnival Clown, *Why Buy a Cow* (Madison)
Cocktail Jokes [vocal by Mack Lewin], *Shaving Cream* [vocal by Paul Wynn] (Cocktail)
Come on Down, *Slow Horses and Fast Women* (Madison)
Disco Dancer, *My Condominium* (Madison)
The Establishment [vocal by Jan Lionel], *What Have I Done* [Benny Bell, as Felix Feifindeckle] (Madison)
Everybody Wants My Fanny, *Wading in the Water* (Vanguard)
The Face on the Bar-Room Floor [recitation by Alan Stewart], *Happy-Go-Lucky Boy* [Stewart] (Madison)
Fido's Wedding, *Doggie Serenade* (Madison)
The Friendly Blackbird, *Laugh Along with Pincus* (Madison)
Hebrew Lessons, *Home Again in Israel* (Zion)
Hey Joe, Two Beers, *How Dry I Am* (Madison)
Home Again, Without Pants, *Yum Yum Yum* (Madison)
Hooray for Me [vocal by Jimmy King], *The Candidates* (Madison)
I'd Rather Do It Myself, *Sweet Violets* (Madison)
Ikey and Mikey, *The Old Canarsie Line* (Madison)
In 1492, What Did Columbus Do? *How Do They Do It?* (Madison)
Jolly Jingles, *Dark Eyes in a Jam* (Madison)
The Junkie's Bible [vocal by Joe Anonymous], *Brooklyn Bridge* (Madison)
Junkie's Lament [vocal by Joe Anonymous], *The Pain of Progress* [Joe Anonymous] (Madison)
Kosher Disco, *Pincus the Peddler* (Madison)
Kosher Hillbilly, *Sweet Violets* (Madison)
Lazy Nellie [Benny Bell and Little Nell], *Dangerous Mike McGee* [Bell, Nell] (Madison)
Meet Me on the Corner [The Ponyboys], *You Know and I Know* [The Ponyboys] (Madison)

Noses, *My Johnny* (Madison)
One Dollar Blues, *Graduation Recitation* (Madison)
Party Songs [vocal by Mack Lewin], *Shaving Cream* [vocal by Paul Wynn]. (Madison)
Pretty Baby [music & lyrics by Kahn-Jackson-Van Arstyne], *Jolly Jingles* (Madison)
Shaving Cream, *More Shaving Cream* (Madison)
Shaving Cream [vocal by Paul Wynn], *The Girl from Chicago* [Wynn] (Madison)
Shaving Cream [vocal by Paul Wynn], *The Girl From Chicago* [Wynn] (Vanguard)
Ship Ahoy, Sailor Boy [vocal by Rose Marie], *You're Not Worth My Tears* [Rose Marie] [music
    & lyrics by Devino, Loder and Richards] (Mercury)
Shish-Ka-Bob, *Brooklyn Bridge* (Madison)
Shish-Ka-Bob, *Six Feet Under* (Madison)
Six Feet Under, *In 1942, What Did Columbus Do* (Madison)
Six Feet Under, *What Did Columbus Do?* (Ariel)
Sweet Violets in Discoland, *Dark Eyes in a Jam* (Madison)
Take a Ship for Yourself [vocal by Paul Wynn], *Baseball Jamboree* [Wynn] (Novelty)
That Magic Melody, *He Done Her Wrong* (Madison)
Till We Meet Again [vocal by the Harmony Dogs] [music by Richard Whiting, lyrics by
    Raymond Eagen], *Brooklyn Bridge* (Madison)
The Turtle Song, *Why Buy a Cow* (Madison)
Washington, Lincoln and Watergate, *A Happy-Go-Lucky Boy* [vocal by Stu Allen] (Madison)

78 rpm records (*side B in italics*)

The Automobile Song, *She's So Clever* (Radio Novelty)
Bar Mitzvah Speech, *Celebration Freylach* [instrumental] (Bell Novelty)
Barnum Was Right, *Meet Me on the Corner* (Bell Novelty)
Benny Blesses a Bride, *A Disgusted Millionaire* (Radio Novelty)
Benny Blesses a Bride, *Misfortune, What Do You Want* (Bell Novelty)
The Boat Song, *A Disgusted Millionaire* (Radio Novelty)
Calypso Mandelbaum, *Song of Peace* (Bell Novelty)
Did You Ever Hear That Song, *Go to Work, You Jerk* (Radio Novelty)
A Disgusted Millionaire, *Elope With Me* (Bell Novelty)
That Dog-Gone-Gone Window, Can't Get It Up Anymore (as Al Driggs), *Living For
    Nothing* [Driggs] (Arrow)
Dopey John, *I Know a Crazy Song* (Radio Novelty)
Down By the Old Mill Stream [music & lyrics by Tell Taylor], *Oh, That Dumbbell* (Bell
    Novelty)
Dr. Yookle Kupvaytig, *No Chiseling* (Bell Novelty)
Eating My Heart Out Over You, *I'm the Guy Who Took a Ship for Himself* (Radio Novelty)
Elope with Me, *A Disgusted Millionaire* (Bell Novelty)
Everybody Wants My Fanny, *How Dry I Am* (Slapstick)
Fancy Definitions, *The Janitor's Can* (Radio Novelty)
Ginger and Spice, *Happiness Fraylach* [instrumental] (Bell Novelty)
The Girl From Atlantic City [as Al Driggs], *Blue Danube* [Johann Strauss] [Eric Gordon
    Band] (Arrow)

The Girl From Baltimore (as Al Driggs), *Forgive Me* [Driggs] (Arrow)
Hebrew Lessons, *Hatikva* [Naphtali Herz Imber] (Zion)
Hetzaleh Getzaleh Goo, *Gelt Gelt Gelt* (Bell Novelty)
Hey Joe, Two Beers, *Pink Pills for Pale People* (Bell)
I Hope They Draft Me Soon, *The Alimony Blues* (Radio Novelty)
I Wish I Were Single Again, *A Warsaw Love Song* (Radio Novelty)
I'll Never Get Drunk Again [as Benny Bimbo], *All On Account of You* [as Theo Lynn]
    (Radio Novelty)
I'm the Guy Who Took a Ship for Myself, *Gone But Not Forgotten* (Radio Novelty)
Johnny's Little Horse [as Al Driggs], *A Son of a Witch [Driggs]* (Arrow)
Living and Laughing, *Hungarian Chodesh* (Bell Novelty)
McCarthy and McGinnis, *Meet Me on the Corner* (Bell Novelty)
Moishe Pipick, *In the Subway* (Bell Novelty)
Mozzel Tuff Far'n M'chitten, *Hebrew School* (Bell Novelty)
My Janitor's Can, *The Automobile Song* (Radio Novelty)
My Mother Said I Shouldn't, *I Had But Fifty Cents* (Radio Novelty)
Nice Little Pussy [as Al Driggs], *If I Do, I Die [Driggs]* (Arrow)
Noses Run in My Family [vocal by Paul Wynn], *Tattooed Lady* [Wynn] (Cocktail)
Our Country Right or Wrong, *We Do It Just the Same* (Radio Novelty)
Oy Could He Dahvin, *Russo-Polski Mazurka* (Bell Novelty)
Pincus Went to the Mountains, *A Disgusted Millionaire* (Bell Novelty)
Pincus the Peddler, *Why Buy a Cow?* (Bell)
Pink Pills for Pale People, *Hey Joe, Two Beers* (Bell Novelty)
Politics, *There Ain't No Santa* (Bell Novelty)
Romania, Romania, *Oy D'Veiber* (Bell Novelty)
Sammy from Miami, *Yum Yum Yum* (Madison)
She's Still Got It, *There Ain't No Santa Claus* (Radio Novelty)
Snow Balls [vocal by Paul Wynn], *I'm the Guy* [Wynn] (Cocktail)
The Son of Pincus the Peddler, *The First Hundred Years* (Bell Novelty)
Sweet Violets, *Hootshe Kootshe* (Radio Novelty)
Take a Ship for Yourself, *Happy Birthday to Love* (Bell Novelty)
Wedding Bells, *Made to Order for Me* (Bell Novelty)
We Do it Just the Same, *Hey Joe, Two Beers* (Bell Novelty)
Yiddish Radio Broadcast, *Wedding Waltz* [instrumental] (Bell Novelty)

ACKNOWLEDGEMENTS

My father, to whom this book is dedicated, retired not long before I began to work on it, and as a retired person with few hobbies and few friends he was only too happy to help me out in many ways. In addition to telling me stories and answering questions, he put together several CD compilations of my grandfather's songs so that I wouldn't have to change 45 rpm record after 45 rpm record. Not only is that time consuming, but I long ago had lost the last of those little doohickeys that you put in the middle of a 45 to keep the musicians from sounding drunk. His contributions are greatly appreciated, and my biggest regret is that he didn't live long enough to see the book published. He tops a long list of people who offered assistance and encouragement in moving the project from wild idea to finished product:

Ben Ohmart, a new friend who is obviously the wisest man in publishing these days; Bill Freytag who, as Nat N. Yahoo, collaborated with me on several rejected proposals and is a constant source of knowledge about the old days in music and recording; Gary Alt, with whom I've been strumming since 1973 on many a musical mission; Bob Buono, my best man, who is incomparable when it comes to moral support; Brian Gari, who invited my father and me to a Friends of Old Time Radio convention, where this book started to take shape; Joe Franklin, one of my grandfather's most loyal fans, and one of this book's earliest supporters; Steve Garrin at VideoActive Productions, who graciously ran interference for me through Joe's incredibly full plate; Dr. Demento and Cousin Bruce Morrow, both of whose efforts revived my grandfather's career, and who each cheered me on in pursuit of my own; Uncle Floyd, my grandfather's favorite accompanist (and in some ways a younger, mildly saner Benny Bell); Rose Marie, who would have been one of my all-time favorites even she didn't record one of my grandfather's songs and then, on my behalf, record her memory of the experience; David Hinckley, who proved that the old tummler still deserved major editorial space; Rollye James, a gracious host who was the first to promise an open door for publicity, sight unseen (but not unheard); Patricia T. O'Connor, who graciously answered a question about the most important line in the book; Ray Toscano, a real *mensch* when it comes to understanding and appreciating why a schnook like me needs a highly-skilled pro like him; the fabulous group at Group M public relations & strategic marketing, Rosemarie Monaco, Jeff Lewis, Jessica Guilfoyle and Magno Parada, who have been consistent in their friendship, advice, technical support and sustenance; Warren Westura, for headshots that make me comfortable having a head; Jim Azarowicz, who exemplifies neighborliness (he helped me out with some of the images for the book, and now I have to take out his garbage for a year); and Becky Copley (and the cast), who brought "Homeless Equity" to life on stage, thereby in a way further endorsing some of my grandfather's creative genes.

Benny Bell, who loved family more than double entendres, would kick me in the candy store if I didn't mention family members who gave him and Molly continued strength through their unconditional love and support, including his son Charley and Charley's daughters Debbie and Laurie and Laurie's daughter Amanda.

And most importantly, my immediate family, all of whom gave me tremendous support: Jeff and Jeannie Bass, who probably still have not fully grasped what kind of crazy family Jeff's sister married into, Steve Levine and his wife, my sister Irene, both great supporters, and she being a primary source of some needed memory-filling-in that renders the famed Elton John affair insignificant; Alaina Levine and Josh Lang, who I will gladly forgive for not wanting "Home Again (Without Pants)" played at their wedding; David Levine, my great internet researcher; my wonderful mom Reneé Samberg, whose kvelling is (almost) every bit as good as royalties; Celia and Dave Stangarone, who continue to bring harmony into our family in more ways than one; Kate Samberg (Brooklyn, USA!) and Dan Samberg (Pasta, USA!), who had the ability and common sense to act relatively normal (most of the time), even during all those times when I didn't; and my best friend and daydream believer, my wife Bonnie: From Oyster Bay to Verona. Who knew? And when we move again, maybe we'll find one of those little doohickeys.

INDEX